Emily Carr

Emily Carr

Doris Shadbolt

Douglas & McIntyre
Vancouver/Toronto

Douglas & McIntyre Ltd.
1615 Venables Street
Vancouver, British Columbia v5L 2H1

Canadian Cataloguing in Publication Data

Shadbolt, Doris, 1918–
   Emily Carr

   Includes bibliographical references.
   ISBN 0-88894-690-2

   1. Carr, Emily, 1871–1945 - Criticism and
interpretation.   2. Painters - Canada - Biography.
I. Carr, Emily, 1871–1945.   II. Title.
ND249.C3S52 1990   759.11   C90-09106105

Typeset in Bembo and Gill by The Typeworks
Printed and bound in Canada by D. W. Friesen & Sons Ltd.
Printed on acid-free paper ∞
Editor: Marilyn Sacks
Designer: George Vaitkunas

We gratefully acknowledge the work of the contributing photographers in this
book, among them Michael Neill, principal photographer for *The Art of Emily
Carr,* many of whose images reappear in this book; Rolfe Bothe, Montreal, for
HAIDA TOTEMS, Q.C.I.; Carlo Catenazzi, Toronto (A.G.O.) for CUMSHEWA;
Brian Merrett, Montreal, for FOREST (tree trunks), and Trevor Mills, Vancouver, for THE CROOKED STAIRCASE, AN INDIAN HOUSE, KOSKIMO VILLAGE,
and THE LONE WATCHER.

Selections from Emily Carr's *Klee Wyck* on page 115 and from her *Hundreds and
Thousands* on pages 79, 170 and 180-81 are reprinted with the permission of Stoddart Publishing Co., Limited, 34 Lesmill Road, Don Mills, Ontario.

The quotation on page 116 from Ralph Pearson's *How To See Modern Pictures* is
reprinted with the permission of Doubleday (Bantam, Doubleday, Dell Publishing Group, Inc.), New York.

Contents

Foreword   6

1 **The Background**   9

2 **Becoming an Artist; Becoming Carr**   25

3 **The Formation of a Mature Style**   45

4 **An Interior Evolution: Belief and Attitudes**   64

5 **The Indian Presence**   83

6 **From Landscape to Nature's Transcendence**   147

Afterword   215

Chronology   219

Notes   223

Maps   228

List of Reproductions   230

Bibliography   234

Acknowledgements   235

Index   236

Foreword

Emily Carr and the National Gallery of Canada first came together in 1927, in the exhibition of *Canadian West Coast Art: Native and Modern* organized by the Gallery's Director Eric Brown and Marius Barbeau of the National Museum of Canada. This ground-breaking exhibition included twenty-six of Emily Carr's innovative and vigorous works.

The exhibition and the artist's visit to eastern Canada that same year were a turning point for Emily Carr: at the age of fifty-six, having worked in relative isolation for so long, she was at last recognized by her artist peers as a great Canadian painter, a pioneering woman, and a spirited, sensitive interpreter of Western Canada.

Doris Shadbolt has here re-examined the life and work of this extraordinary woman. Her book accompanies the National Gallery's exhibition in the summer of 1990, the first major retrospective of the art of Emily Carr since 1971. By happy coincidence, and some design, the book and the exhibition come together on the twentieth anniversary of the Report of the Royal Commission on the Status of Women in Canada, published in 1970. I am delighted that we—the National Gallery, Doris Shadbolt, and Douglas & McIntyre, the publishers—are able to honour the achievements of Emily Carr, and to present them to the people of Canada.

The Gallery gratefully acknowledges the generous assistance of American Express Canada, Inc., which has made the exhibition possible. Our warmest thanks.

Dr. Shirley L. Thomson
Director, National Gallery of Canada

"A mind forever voyaging through strange seas of thought alone."
—William Wordsworth

American Express Canada, Inc. is proud to be a partner with the National Gallery of Canada in presenting a retrospective of Emily Carr's work. The broad range of more than 150 works includes Carr's lively early studies of the Queen Charlotte Islands and northern British Columbia native villages, to the reflective later paintings like ABOVE THE TREES.

We believe that this exhibition, curated by Doris Shadbolt, is a fitting tribute to a woman of singular determination and artistic ability, who stretched the boundaries of conventional wisdom and thought.

We hope many Canadians will enjoy the Emily Carr exhibition and share this priceless record of Canadian art.

Morris A. Perlis
President and General Manager
American Express Canada, Inc.

SELF PORTRAIT 1938–39
Oil on paper, 86.36 x 58.42 cm
Private collection

1 The Background

Forty-five years after Emily Carr's death, as the retrospective view of her artistic output lengthens and the angle of our vision widens, her inseparability from the broad current of this century's modern art is confirmed; but so also is her northern-ness, her willed Canadian-ness, her Pacific West Coast-ness, and her striking individual otherness.

The story of modern art since the final quarter of the last century has been, for the most part, that of artists working with a special sense of purpose, conscious that they were giving art a new definition and reshaping its role in society. Of the artists who have a place in that story, many worked out of cultural milieus that readily gave them a familiarity with the art movements of their time and that enabled them to see themselves as part of history in the making. Close contemporaries of Carr in Europe—where at one period in her life she went to further her art—with whose work it could be claimed she had some if only fleeting or unknowing kinship such as Matisse, Vlaminck, Marquet, Rouault, Dufy, Marc and Kandinsky, were born into older cultures having strong artistic traditions capable of providing their artists with a starting base or, alternatively, an anchor point for departure. Even when they grew up in small provincial towns it was not too difficult, given the short distances separating European urban centres, to move within reach of a community of pacemaking peers who would provide the atmosphere of dialogue, idea exchange and critical awareness in which art thrives.

Carr's cultural background was that of the "new world"— a very new world—and in her day restricted mobility and problems of communication made contact with centres of artistic sophistication, even within Canada, special events rather than everyday assumptions. She did make such contacts with the larger stream of art as the development of her work demanded, but she never really wanted to be part of a close community of artists, even though she frequently complained of the absence of "real" artists in her home city. Temperamentally she was a solitary, like other of her northern, and to her unknown, contemporaries such as Edvard Munch or Ferdinand Hodler, needing her geographic isolation, and accepting the natural cultural vacuity of a town not too removed from its frontier days.

Carr's British Columbia

Emily Carr was born in Victoria on Vancouver Island in the province of British Columbia 3 December 1871, died there 2 March 1945, and lived most of her life within a few blocks of the house where she was born. In her lifetime she travelled by rail back and forth across the broad reach of Canada twice on her way to Europe, and three times more to its eastern centres, so that she had some passing experience of the vast dimension of space, the great gaps between clusters of habitation, the geographical richness and variety which were insistent characteristics of her natal country. Although she could not have grasped the extent of uninhabited northern wilderness, never having had the opportunity to observe it from the air, her travels in her own province in search of native Indian material ensured that she was not lacking in the experience of hinterland. Yet she was not possessed of the restless traveller's curiosity about other parts of Canada or North America, or of the world. Her instincts were homing and her all-fulfilling intimacy was with British Columbia where she was born, where her imaginative roots as a child were nourished and where she carried out her life's work. She lived in a time when patriotism was strong and in due course she was able to translate her passionate attachment to one particular part of Canada into a fierce and broader Canadianism as well.

Canada's most westerly province on the Pacific coast is larger than the United Kingdom, France, the Netherlands, Belgium and Switzerland combined with a landscape of impressive scale and physical variety and a long coastline of convoluted complexity. Running parallel to the southern mainland is Vancouver Island, where the capital Victoria is situated, the largest island on the west coast of North America and itself bigger than England. The province is physically distanced from eastern centres of population in Canada (or the United States) by great stretches of prairie and barricaded on its eastern border by the formidable range of the Rocky mountains, while on its western edge the Pacific Ocean is another distancing presence.

The last part of the country in North America to be effectively settled and developed, British Columbia has had a brief history; less than a century and a half ago it was the domain of native Indians and the hunting terrain of foreign fur traders. The British, whose explorers of this land in the eighteenth century won out against those of other acquisitive nations such as Spain, Russia and France, gained sovereignty over the territory north of the forty-ninth parallel. In 1849 they made a colony of Vancouver Island, a measure calculated to reserve its rich resources of timber and gold for the British Empire and its ample space and opportunities for British settlers while preventing American migration northward up the Pacific coast from California. The encouragement of British emigration succeeded so well that it was not until 1941 that the Canadian-born outnumbered the British-born in the province.[1]

It was only in 1871, the year of Carr's birth, that British Columbia changed its status from that of a colony of the Empire and became a province within the Canadian Federation, a political restructuring which did nothing to alter the pervasive and determined Britishizing of the new country. A condition of amalgamation had been the extension of the Canadian Pacific Railway through the Rocky Mountains to the West Coast, and the arrival in Vancouver in 1886 of the first trans-Canada train from the East did indeed herald the beginning of better communication with the rest of the nation. Nonetheless, British Columbia was then, as it still remains today to some degree, a region politically and culturally distinct from the rest of Canada, isolated by distance and distinguished perhaps above all by the force of its geography.

Small's Victoria[2]

Carr was born to English parents who came to Victoria in 1863. Her father had put behind him his adventurous youth to become a solid Victoria citizen operating a prosperous business in wholesale groceries and liquors and providing a comfortable, well-run household for his family of five daughters and a son. (The latter died at the age of twenty-three and three other sons had died in infancy.) With its population of less than eight thousand at the time of Carr's birth, Victoria, though the site of government, by the mid-1870s had lost its place of prominence to Vancouver, the larger, more vital and better connected centre of the new and rapidly growing province. Vancouver Island was removed from the mainland by a five- or six-hour ferry ride and was thus in a special position of remoteness from the rest of Canada.

The gold rush to the interior of the province in 1858, which had channelled itself through Victoria making it for several years a bustling and chaotic frontier town with a mix of many nationalities, entrepreneurial businesses and social elements, was over by the seventies and eighties when Carr was growing up. The Victoria of her childhood had already settled into the more stable community of dominant British tone which is described—with contempt—in her written reminiscences of those early years. "Old Victoria" did its best to project the social, political and cultural values of the Britain whose Queen had given the city her name. British settlers—Scottish, Irish and Welsh as well as English—held the official posts, comprised the professional element and generally ran affairs. They and their friends and relatives brought with them zealously guarded ways, customs and notions of how things should be done, to say nothing of their cherished possessions: china, furniture, heirlooms. Carr tells of her "ultra-English" father who "thought everything English was much better than anything Canadian."[3]

The British set the moral and social tone, and at the level of polite sociability—official functions, the Governor's balls and tea parties, private clubs and schools and church socials—the city must have seemed much like a community in Britain. The gentle climate and sea air (so similar to that in pockets of England), which had helped attract British settlers to begin with, contributed to the genteel and leisurely way of life possible for those with some means as did the availablity of cheap Chinese and native Indian help. The Carr household included Bong, a Chinese day servant and the Indian "Wash Mary" who looked after the laundry.

Needless to say, Victoria's Englishness, being the result of transplanted attitudes and mores rather than of the centuries of slow evolution on which its model rested, left a cultural vacuum beneath its surface which the city was too young to fill. The province's history was at too close range to have distilled any nurturing myths, and too chaotic to have produced any popular heroes or grand events capable of unifying the community's imagination in a sense of its own destiny. The veneer of British gentility was equally unsubstantiated by authoritative institutions of learning or culture. It was a community without a university and lacked the general ferment of ideas and intellectual activity found in longer settled, more cosmopolitan centres. During Carr's adolescent years there was really no one in Victoria to stimulate and lead her or even to fully understand her demanding and increasingly complex imaginative needs; she was alone in the things that mattered to her most, a predicament that characterized much of her life. The fact of being born a woman in a society shaped to maintain the control of men was one which had to be faced early since she was a child of strong will and free spirit confronted by an authoritarian father who was the unquestioned head of the household. Her final achievement as an artist of independent vision was accomplished in full awareness of the odds against her as a woman painter. Her decision to remain unmarried, though she attracted men and had at least one serious suitor, rested in part on her awareness that her mandatory role as wife and mother would deny her more urgent artist's demands.

In the stories written as an adult, the child Carr repeatedly rails against the Victorianism of many fellow Victorians, particularly those whom she felt exhibited social or moral pretensions: their self-satisfied earnestness, callow complacency, false modesty; their substitution of politesse for naturalness and the expression of real feelings. (She herself, of course, was Victorian in more ways than she knew, such as her puritanical attitude to sex.) Finally, her irritation with the false claim to so much Britishness helped her to a realization of Canadian-ness. Assuming an ardently Canadian rather than an old-world outlook became important morally and artistically for Carr, a stance delineated— as it would be so often in her life—by intense reaction against a negative situation.

Old Victoria may have been in many ways a backwater, but in others it was a paradise for a child whose intellectual demands were not yet too advanced. There was first forged the deep bond with nature that was to become the wellspring of her art and her life's sustaining centre, and there she first touched the subject material that was to lead her to the second great source and theme of her art, the native Indian presence and heritage.

Insistent and abundant nature was an inescapable condition of life in Victoria and its environs. The small Emily was particularly fortunate in having ready access to nature's riches, for through the back fence of the semi-rural family property she could easily reach the extensive near wildness of Beacon Hill Park with its native flowers and luxuriant growth. There too were the cliffs and below them the giant driftwood-strewn beaches and rocky crenelated foreshore, the sweeping views of the broad blue Strait of Juan de Fuca and beyond that the profile of the Cascade Moun- tains on the American coast. Seemingly endless variations on such configurations of mountains, tree-clad hills, waters of this or that bay or inlet could be found by travelling a kilometre or so in any direction. Within short distances were enormous stands of virgin trees—cedar, fir, pine as well as many of the deciduous trees she loved. And always within touch was the more intimate growth of smaller forms—grasses, flowers, bushes, wild or garden variety—for growth is irrepressible in Victoria's mild climate.

It would be a mistake to omit animals from the list of Carr's early immersion in nature. The family's cow became the occasion of one of her stories in *The Book of Small*, and in *Growing Pains* she links her love of animals and nature in acknowledging her debt to "Johnny," the former circus pony who provided her with a means of getting away from town to "the deep lovely places that were the very foundation on which my work as a painter was to be built."[4] Her early passion for animals continued all her life, providing her for a time with a source of income (she bred dogs), and always with the comfort and pleasure of their company. Animals—birds, dogs, rats, a monkey—filled her house, which at times became a veritable menagerie, and she almost always took one or more with her on her travels. They added to the proper Victorians' perception of her as an eccentric, but for her, animals were simply a manifestation of the mystery and joy of living things.

The roots of Carr's second preoccupying painting theme also go back to her childhood, a time when there were numerous active native Indian reserves on Vancouver Island and in the lower mainland of the province. That of the Songhees, a division of the Coast Salish people, was just across the harbour from Victoria. Their canoes were commonly seen being paddled in the harbour or drawn up at the wharves where their owners sold fish, berries or handsome handwoven baskets, products they also peddled from door to door. And, writes the young Emily, "frequently [they] camped round on the beaches in the course of their travels up and down the coast in their great canoes and often I used to wish I had been born an Indian."[5] It was through an exchange of baskets for old clothes that Carr met Sophie Frank, a North Vancouver Indian who became a lifelong friend. She and other natives whom Carr met in the course of her travels appear frequently in her stories and journals. The Indians who were so much a part of the Victoria scene had, through the white people's effective takeover of their lands and destruction of their life-style, lost the dignity of their traditional culture. They existed outside the conventional society of Victoria and were generally looked down upon or at best condescended to. Carr records an act of her merchant father who, in a surprising gesture of generosity, distributed cases of Malaga raisins to Indian women come to trade at his store. When queried he admitted that the raisins were full of maggots which, according to him, the Indians did not at all mind.[6] The natives' plight as outcasts from conventional society only made them potentially more appealing to Carr since she felt herself to be something of a social misfit. Their unassimilated presence in her environment fascinated her, and served as an introduction which would lead to her discovery of the great monumental carvings of their northern cousins.

Victoria's Art Scene

The story of Canadian art commences as that of a new-world country modestly reflecting its dual colonial origins, French and English, and then gradually, as political and economic growth became consolidated, wading tentatively into the mainstream of European and finally American art. Perhaps because of its lack of urban concentration, Canada has never been in the forefront of major art movements, which have always originated in other countries, and which have only appeared in Canadian art practice after a time lag (admittedly of diminished duration since the advent of the electronic age). But Canadians know well that the larger Canadian art story, centred in the metropolitan areas of Ontario and Quebec, contains at least half a dozen other particular histories as is inevitable in a vast country whose varying geographies, immigration policies and political and economic patterns give rise to diverse cultures. British Columbia has one of those histories and, for obvious reasons of delayed development, it started with the longest time lag.

Given the general cultural context of Victoria when Carr was growing into adulthood in the 1870s and eighties, the city could not be expected to reflect in its attitudes or activities any notion of art as a consuming vocation for serious people or as a necessary function of society. Insofar as the word "art" meant anything at all to average educated citizens, it probably conjured up Victorian or other images brought with them from the "old country." Even if the information had been available, there were no up-to-date art circles to get excited over the work being done by the Impressionist painters in France in the 1870s, or even over painting in eastern Canada where the scene was more developed than in the West.

This is not to say that Victoria did not have its own kind of unpretentious art activity, the emphasis being often on the activity rather than the art. There had been amateur and professional artists from the time of the early explorers: traders made visual documents or topographical records, and in the 1880s, with the settlement of the area already well under way, artists from eastern

Canada and abroad began to visit, eager to depict the new country, its native Indians and its stunning scenery. With the completion of the Canadian Pacific Railway in 1885, a wave of artists from eastern Canada—F. M. Bell-Smith, Lucius O'Brien, T. Mower Martin, J. A. Fraser and others—began making trips to the West Coast, encouraged by the railway's offer of free passes and the possibility of a commission. Sometimes their visits included Vancouver Island and a stop in Victoria, the only city of any size there. Essentially they were tourist artists exploiting the local scenery; their talents and their products were intended for eastern consumption and they contributed little or nothing to the enrichment of the local art scene.

Although Carr could claim that her family had never produced an artist, nor even known one, the idea of art as a social accomplishment and an acceptable leisure activity, especially for young ladies, like piano playing was common enough in her childhood. She was allowed to take drawing lessons as a child and again in her mid-teens once a week at a Victoria high school after the regular classes.

By the end of the century an interest in art was shared by enough people in Victoria and Vancouver to encourage the formation of sketching groups and exhibiting societies. Fall fairs in Victoria included art displays alongside the exhibits of livestock and agricultural, industrial and other products that made up these annual events, and it was in such a context in 1894 that Carr's work was first shown on her return from school in San Francisco. The Island Art Club, which held its first exhibition in 1910, became the Island Arts and Crafts Club, and finally the Island Arts and Crafts Society, an organization on which she was to vent much scorn. Its members, whose reasons for joining were often partly social (their annual exhibition was one of the major social events of the year), were limited in their notion of art and usually amateur in attitude however skilled they were in the naturalistic depiction of their subjects. The lists of exhibitors in the early years of the IACS—composed largely of female names—shows the degree to which art was a woman's activity, thereby indicating the minor importance it was accorded. Most of the artists were steeped in the British watercolour tradition; they were distant and adulterated artistic descendants of the Norwich school of painters who had infused their observation and love of the English countryside with a touch of sturdy Dutch naturalism. Carr herself would produce in this mode until she was well into her thirties, in her case not for lack of serious intent but rather from an absence of artistic reference points and support structures within her reach. Mention should be made of Sophie Pemberton, a close contemporary of Carr who had training at the Slade School of Art in London and was a serious painter. Her work, however, was not challenging enough to raise the level of local awareness though she herself was to help Carr indirectly later on.

In 1939, in a letter to the director of the National Gallery of Canada, Carr complained of Victoria "as the most hopeless place in the Dominion" and of the IACS as a "necklace of millstones around the neck of art. . . ."[7] Still, despite her contempt she continued to exhibit with them until 1937. She often supplemented what few public exhibiting opportunities there were in Victoria with shows in her own studio, and for a time in the 1930s she had hopes of converting the main floor of her house into a people's gallery financed by public subscription. In 1930 she had an exhibition, sponsored by the Women's Canadian Club, in Victoria's Crystal Gardens (a swimming pool with connected tea lounge that could be used as gallery space) which lasted several days. An offer by a citizen of funds for a public gallery, contingent on the city's acceptance of his private collection, was turned down in 1929. There still was no public gallery when Carr died in 1945, a situation that resulted in the Emily Carr Trust Collection of works going to the Vancouver Art Gallery.

Mainland Vancouver by the first decade of the century had a little more to offer artists, and Carr exhibited in its Studio Club. She taught classes in the city between 1905 and 1909 and at the end of that year became a member of the British Columbia Society of Fine Arts, the first chartered art society in the province, a status which conferred a more professional tone on its shows. By 1925 that city had an art school which brought in as teachers from eastern Canada such highly respected artists as F. H. Varley and J. W. G. Macdonald, and by 1931 it had a civic gallery and a growing number of serious professional artists with whom Carr would share her work in the Gallery's annual juried exhibitions and other group shows. In 1938 she had her first solo show at the Vancouver Art Gallery, an event she repeated almost every year until her death, calling these exhibitions her "annuals." (At that time any artist could apply for space for which a small rental fee was paid.)

Showing her work in home territory on the West Coast of the country was always important to Carr who, like any artist, needed the reality of close-range response; moreover, she was very much a hometown person to whom the goodwill of the people she lived among was more important "than the praise of the whole world."[8] Of course even this exposure was very limited in what it could do for her. The power centres for Canadian art were in the older eastern cities where a serious climate for art had long existed and where innovative artists could show their work in various clubs, societies and galleries amid an atmosphere of lively discussion. Once Carr came to the attention of influential artists and officials there, as she did in 1927, Victoria's backward-ness became less stifling for her. At that point she began to partic-ipate in exhibitions of more than local or regional significance and increasingly on the basis of invitation rather than self-created opportunity. She exhibited with the most advanced artists' group in English-speaking Canada, the Group of Seven, in eastern Canada in 1930 and 1931; with its successor, the Canadian Group of Painters, and occasionally with the Ontario Society of Artists. She participated in a women's international exhibition in Detroit in 1929 and in exhibitions of Canadian art circulated by the National Gallery which were shown in Washington, D.C., and other American cities during the early thirties. In 1930 she had an exhibition at the Art Institute of Seattle; in 1933 she was repre-sented in an international exhibition of women artists in Amsterdam, and in 1937 she had paintings shown in London and Paris. In 1935 and 1937 she had solo shows in Toronto, the first at the Lyceum Club and Women's Art Association, the second at the University of Toronto's Hart House. And so, in her sixties, with her work shown in contexts where it could be recognized for its strength and individuality, and commented on by persons of respected critical opinion such as Eric Newton, critic of the *Manchester Guardian* in England, or G. Campbell McInnes of Toronto, she became an established part of the larger Canadian art scene, visited by travelling celebrities and notables even while maintaining her essential position as a loner "on the edge of nowhere."[9]

Having such improved contacts for her art outside Victoria did not leave Carr without real problems in maintaining the connections that had been established. Her letters to art officials and friends in the thirties remind us how thinly stretched the Canadian art scene was, how centred in the eastern cities, how isolated the West Coast, how tenuous the communication between regions, how culturally lonely the entire country. They underline the vital role the art societies (really exhibiting societies) had to play—even with their entanglements of personal jealousies and ambitions—in the absence of an adequate dealer system for contemporary art. The letters recall a time when a few major art institutions were trying to serve a vast nation while local or regional ones often operated on a semi-amateur basis, as affairs between well-meaning friends. She reminds us of the practical frustrations of being an aging female artist distant from the centre: the expense and sheer fatigue of crating up one's work for shipment to eastern Canada, or even across the water to Vancouver; of being outside the information flow and so being notified at the last moment or too late of an important show in Toronto; of the absence on the West Coast of good criticism or an informed and enquiring public.

Her work, though seen in the United States and several countries in Europe and even singled out for comment once or twice, was no more sought after outside her own country in her own day than was that of the Canadian contemporaries with whom she exhibited. Explanations are not too difficult to find. The sponsoring organizations of travelling exhibitions in which she took part too often lacked the artistic credibility to attract critical attention within the hosting country; or, as in the case of the National Gallery, the exhibitions they sponsored abroad could be viewed by the critical community as official cultural propaganda. More realistically, the art of English Canada, whatever its intrinsic quality, tended to be seen as that of a colonial society and, in truth, in Carr's time it was not in the advanced stream of international modern art flowing out of Europe and then from the United States.

The Carr Revealed in Her Writing

Questions of talent aside, a woman of Carr's generation and social and cultural background had to have exceptional qualities of determination and strength to reach the high level of her accomplishment. Her writing stands on its own and has gained her an enthusiastic audience that quantitatively outstrips interest in her painting; but it also tells us much about the woman behind the art. Many artists keep journals, write essays about art, write poetry, but rarely do they give us such a full picture of themselves as Emily Carr has in her writing. The saying "How do I know what I think till I see what I've said" might well have been coined for her, for she was constantly seeking to clarify her thoughts through jotting down ideas and feelings in her notebooks or journals. Writing was a compulsive form of expression for her, as compulsive as painting and less physically depleting.

There are five books of her stories and reminiscences, all essentially autobiographical in nature and all written some years after the events they describe. Although notes about them were often made many years ahead of the stories, the inevitable blurring and conscious or unconscious reconstructing habit of memory has affected their factual reliability; so of course has the conscious storyteller in her, altering situations and exaggerating characters for literary effect. Still, they refer to real situations and events and can probably be relied on as valid records of feeling.[10] *The Book of Small* speaks of an imaginative child's enchanted, disciplined and protected childhood in "Victorian" Victoria. The strong note of rebellion, the sense of being the wilful other (and not displeased to be so) among conformists is already there, a note that becomes a refrain in *The House of All Sorts* and *Growing Pains*. The former tells of her frustrations and her tenants' unreasonableness during the years of infrequent painting when she rented rooms in her small apartment house; the latter is subtitled "The Autobiography of Emily Carr," but it is rather a collection of short pieces recalling episodes and periods of her life without any attempt to connect them in continuous time. Being the individual she needed to be, shaking off the conservative Victorianism she had inherited, involved the appearance of eccentricity in small ways (her singular manner of dress, her passionate love of animals, her outspokenness) and finally in the big way of her art which had to become large and free and determinedly "Canadian," and that meant "non-Victorian." The undertone of modesty and self-deprecation which surfaces from time to time is only the flip side of the coin that emphasizes its face—her strength, her sense of self. *Klee Wyck,* in which she looks back on her experiences with Indians and her visits to Indian communities, gives us an image of the fully engaged, self-forgetting artist, "fighting" her way through to her subjects, responding intensely and openly to their messages. The rebelliousness of the child and the sometimes self-conscious unconventionality of the adult have become the tough fibre of the woman artist totally given over to her demanding and compelling artist's struggle.

The artist that we deduce behind the Klee Wyck stories speaks out directly in *Hundreds and Thousands,* the published Journals which Carr started in 1927 at the age of fifty-six and kept until 1941, four years before her death. Here we get the mature artist who has found herself but whose continuing pursuit of life and art's ultimate mysteries were all the more intense for the lateness of her arrival. On one level they provide a partial account of activities: her trips to Toronto and Chicago; her sketching sessions in the countryside near Victoria; her successes or disappointments in the world of exhibitions and sales; her social life with family and friends. But they are most valuable because in them she talks spontaneously and passionately about her art and her spirituality—her painful struggles and her moments of elation—revealing the knowledgeable painter and her working methods, her rootedness in all of nature, the interconnectedness of her intention for her art and her search for religious meaning in life. The Journals are in fact a personal manifesto, a passionate confession of artistic faith. The "hundreds and thousands" of her title, refers to tiny English candies, so small that they must be consumed by the mouthful to be appreciated, a not inappropriate thought when referring to a person who has her homey domestic side but who prefers life in big gulps, not dainty bites.

And there is the voluminous output of the obsessive letter-writing Carr, who knew that "there is a side of friendship that develops better and stronger by correspondence than contact, especially with some people who can get their thoughts clearer when they see them written. . . [and when] that beastliness, self-consciousness, is left out. . . . "[11] More and more of the letters are finding their way into public collections where, depending on her relationship to the correspondent, they tell of Carr the highly practical person dealing with the decisions and arrangements required in daily life, the earthy and excruciatingly funny Carr clowning with word images, the compulsive communicator whose words tumble out in a mad rush, the sociable being who enjoys neighbourly gossip and small talk, the irrascible older woman whose patience wears thin when art officials prove delinquent in their supposed responsibilities or when someone just rubs her the wrong way.

Unfortunately the only letters in which she spoke from the heart about artistic or spiritual things were the many written to, but not kept by, Lawren Harris, a leading Canadian artist who became the most important single influence in her artistic life. We know by implication from his letters to her, and from her comment made many years later, that the exchange was about work, "almost all work, one artist to another."[12] There are many letters written to Ira Dilworth, who brought her first book to the attention of Oxford University Press, edited all her later manuscripts, and at her death became one of the trustees of her estate and her literary executor. Written in her later years, they record her failing health and loneliness once the compelling drive of her art could no longer fill her life. But, interestingly, she structures the correspondence according to the ambivalence she was always aware of in her personality, splitting herself into two personae: Small (the title of the book about her childhood), the free imaginative child spirit in her, and Emily, the pragmatic, and self-admittedly sometimes uncharitable self. Both selves were necessary to her artistic life, and her recognition of their ambivalence permitted her to swing productively from one to the other.

The books consciously written for publication, the letters, and the journals answered different needs for Carr: the books to substantiate the self-image she needed to authorize her life and art (*Small, Growing Pains, The House of All Sorts*); the letters for the comfortable day-to-day warmth of friendship beyond the actual social occasions with family and friends (which she could take in only limited amounts); the journals for the working out and clarification of her artistic and spiritual goals. The substance of the three forms is quite separate with little overlapping, and that pattern is revealing. She could talk to others about the externals of art—the mechanics, the system, even the gossip—but about its deepest meanings and problems she talked only to herself. There were caring friends near her in Victoria but never a group of artist peers with whom to exchange ideas. She complained about that particular aloneness from time to time, but the truth is that she needed their absence more than their presence; her art was too deeply lodged within herself for discussion. That is the real essence of Carr's isolation.

2 Becoming an Artist; Becoming Carr

The process by which artists mature and find themselves in their art—essentially a matter of internal assimilation to which such questions as skill and technique are secondary—is a long one. They may produce admirable work as their talents emerge, but there comes a point (often visible only with a measure of retrospection) when they become themselves in their art: influences absorbed, the complex factors of creativity in working alignment, full potential activated. Emily Carr produced a large body of work in her long years of artistic incompleteness, all of it technically competent and increasingly knowledgeable, much of it reflecting venturesomeness in one or another aspect. But not until she was about forty was she able to free herself from the artistic Victorianism that she had inherited, and not until her late fifties could she be said to have *become Carr in her art*. As observers of the external narrative, we could say that there were three stages in her artist's progress towards maturity. The first, involving study in San Francisco and England, gave her some painting skills and practice and confirmed her stance as a serious artist. The second took her to France where she successfully left behind her old-world painter's eyes, mastered a modern approach to painting and produced some strikingly fine works. There she made a major advance even though, as it turned out, it did not take her in the direction she was destined to go. The third was generated by a several-week trip to eastern Canada where she

participated in a significant exhibition and met a group of prominent Ontario artists. This event, though brief, precipitated a
climactic change in her life and art and propelled her into full and
vigorous, if belated, artistic fulfilment.

San Francisco

Although the first stage of Carr's artist's progress lasted a long
time and covers a period of considerable interest to her biog-
raphers, it can be dealt with fairly summarily here since, apart
from demonstrating her seriousness and will to succeed, little of
Carr's exceptional artist's potential was released. In the late
summer of 1890 she went south to attend the California School of
Design in San Francisco, then located in dilapitated quarters on
Pine Street over the old public market. The school, founded in
1874, was thriving but conservative, and teaching followed the
conventions of the time. Its director, A. F. Mathews, had recently
come from five years of study at the Académie Julian in Paris, but
neither his teaching nor his own painting reflected the more
advanced art then being produced in France. Emily took his class
in drawing from antique models but not his life class, for the
prudishness of her upbringing was such that she could not face
the nude models. Writing about those days many years later, she
recalled her teacher in still life painting, the "French Professor"
(Amédée Jouillin), who told her she had good colour sense, and
who by commanding her to "scrape" her canvas and "scrape
again" attempted to "torment" her into a spirited rather than
tentative approach to painting.[1] Of all the classes she liked best the
optional weekly outdoor sketching sessions in vacant lots, cow
pastures or among stretches of fence and bush. "Sketching outdoors was a fluid process, half-looking, half dreaming, awaiting
invitation from the spirit of the subject to 'come, meet me half
way.'. . . Atmosphere, space cannot be touched, bullied like the
vegetables of still life or like the plaster casts. These space things
asked to be felt not with finger-tips but with one's whole self."[2]
Unfortunately, none of those early outdoor efforts remain to tell
us whether she was indeed sketching from her "whole self" or
whether, as is more likely, she was simply projecting on her
remembered youth the wisdom of her later experience as a sea-
soned artist.

The hovering presence of family and their chaperoning friends in San Francisco kept her safely within the social ambience of Victorian propriety where contact with more culturally liberated circles was not likely to occur. As she later recalled, "San Francisco did not have much to offer in the way of art study other than the school itself, no galleries, no picture exhibitions. Art was just beginning out west. The School was new."[3] In fact, it had been established sixteen years before as the teaching appendage of the San Francisco Art Association; it held annual exhibitions, which she must have seen, and certainly there were other exhibiting venues in the city. But there is no evidence that Carr took advantage of the richer artistic milieu around her. Although she did not lack the courage to take decisive and independent action to further her art (by travelling to major art centres to study), she was not equipped either by temperament or early conditioning to take advantage, once in those centres, of the full range of artistic experience they had to offer. Throughout her life she remained timid and uncomfortable in company which she felt to be more intellectually sophisticated than she was except where the relationship could be interpreted as that of master and pupil, mentor and follower. Even when the opportunity presented itself, she never ventured to penetrate even the fringes of artists'—let alone bohemian artists'—circles unless she was following someone else's lead.

Carr returned to Victoria in the fall of 1893 after three years and a few months in San Francisco. She had learned the basics of her craft as they were then understood; not too many examples of her school work can be identified, but there are a few paintings to show that she knew how to compose a still life or a flower piece and to handle tonal colour in convincing representations of her subjects. Her own description of the work she brought back with her seems accurate enough: "humdrum and unemotional—objects honestly portrayed, nothing more,"[4] and this evaluation could also be applied to drawings and watercolours she did during the next few years back in Victoria. Nothing had happened at the California school to give her a vision of what art might be for her—nothing at least that showed in her work.

London/England

In the late summer of 1899 she set out for London, having saved
enough money from the children's classes she had organized in
Victoria and taught with considerable success after her return
from San Francisco. England was chosen over France partly
because there was no language problem but more likely because it
was a choice that her sisters—whose moral support she still
needed—would countenance. It was an unfortunate choice.
Although London was rich in museums and exhibitions where art
history and the old masters could be studied, it was not an active
centre of advanced art production. British art was still following a
traditional course at the end of the 1800s and during the first
decades of the 1900s, and it was French rather than English
painters who picked up on Constable's brilliant pictorial signal to
modernism. In England the influence of Impressionism was
belated and watered-down, and not until the critic Roger Fry
organized two historic exhibitions at the Grafton Galleries in
1910–11 and 1912 did the situation begin to change. The first
included 150 works by Manet, Cézanne, Gauguin, Van Gogh and
the French symbolists; the second began with Cézanne and placed
the emphasis on Matisse and the Fauves, Picasso and the Cubists.
Only after the impact of those shows did English art begin to stir
out of its general conservatism, too late to provide a similar service for Carr when she was in England. At the time of Fry's first
exhibition Carr was in France making her own acquaintance with
the Post-Impressionist vision.

   The Westminster School of Art, which Carr entered in the fall
of 1899, a school under the aegis of the narrow-minded Royal
Academy, was plodding and uninspired and its atmosphere
inhibitingly formal. An obsessed student, she followed the day-
long life classes (her prudery now overcome) with evening classes
in design, anatomy and clay modelling. More enjoyable and
probably useful to her art were escapes to the country from
London whose "oldness and history . . . made little appeal to
me. . . . cities did not sit on me comfortably."[5] There was a
summer vacation in Berkshire where she joined a class and had
her first outdoor sketching experience in England. Looking back
she believed she had learned a lot there where the distances were
softened by haze and the "colour did not throb so violently."[6]

The most artistically helpful time of all her largely unhappy and unprofitable stay in England was spent from August to late winter of 1901–2 in St. Ives, Cornwall, where she sought out the studio of the half-Swedish Julius Olsson, a painter of impressionistic seascapes. There she was part of an informal class of ten or so students of various ages where her own thirty-one years were not too conspicuous. Olsson's views and approaches differed from those of his teaching partner Algernon Talmage, an admirer of Constable and a painter of lyrical meadow scenes. The energetic Olsson wanted his students to paint the white boats and the sea, working with full sunlight on the canvas. Talmage, whom Carr found more sympathetic, respected her preference for the gentle places such as those she found in the ivy-draped Tregenna Wood behind the village.

In the spring of 1902 she went to the Meadows Studios in Bushey, Hertfordshire, where "the land dipped and rose pastorally and was dotted with sheep, cows and spreads of bluebells. Everything was yellow-green and pearly with young spring. Larks hurried up to Heaven as if late for choir practice."[7] There she also painted in a small wood, and her teacher, John Whiteley, a conservative but sensitive watercolour painter of landscape and the figure, left her with an important lesson: "The coming and going of foliage is more than just flat pattern. . . ." That observation tallied well with Talmage's words: "there is sunshine too in the shadows."[8] These two lessons on the observation of nature, and a growing realization that her longstanding response to nature would somehow have to be at the core of her art, were probably the most significant effects of Carr's five-year stay in England.

There remains a slight but delightful untitled little watercolour of a big sky and meadow with an umbrella-protected picnicker or sketcher seated on its green expanse. This is probably a note from one of Carr's happy excursions into the English countryside, very likely Bushey. For the most part the paintings done in England have largely disappeared, most of them destroyed many years after her return to Victoria when she was clearing out her past.

Her stay in England almost from the beginning was marred by various physical ailments which interrupted her work, and the last eighteen months were spent miserably in a Suffolk sanatorium where she was seriously ill. She arrived back in Victoria in mid–October 1904 having spent a month visiting friends on their ranch in the cattle range country of central British Columbia. The English sojourn had not advanced her art, but neither had it shaken her purposefulness about art. Of the five-and-a-half years following her return, mostly spent teaching and painting quietly in Vancouver (or in Victoria on weekends), a passing mention should be made here of the commencement of her serious interest in native Indian art which by her own account began in 1907.

France and the New Art

A visit to France in 1910–11 marks Carr's effective break with Victorian concepts of art and the old-world sensibility she had been immersed in for so long. France had been a prime lure for artists from the United States for quite some time, and for artists from eastern Canada since the latter quarter of the nineteenth century. Carr's objective in setting out for France was clear to her: to search out "this New Art." She wrote, "I heard it ridiculed, praised, liked, hated. Something in it stirred me but I could not at first make head or tail of what it was all about. I saw at once that it made recent conservative painting look flavourless, little, unconvincing."[9] What her contact with the "new art" had been, or indeed what she had in mind as she set out for France on 10 July 1910, remains a matter of speculation; her words written many years later refer to something she had seen or heard discussed in Victoria or more likely Vancouver. In any case, they reflect a general urge to seek fresh inspiration in the then world's art capital.

Artistic Paris during the years 1907–12 was in a state of excited discovery, its advancing edge well launched into the sea of modernity as the notion of abstract art was explored in a variety of ways. At the time of Carr's arrival Picasso and Braque were painting their "facet" cubist pictures and the following summer would work out a flatly patterned Cubism. In 1911 the Cubists would make group demonstrations at the Salon des Indépendants and Salon d'Automne exhibitions in Paris and in a large cubist exhibition in Brussels. Their numbers included Fernand Léger (with whose cubist work Carr's would some years later show an affinity) and a new recruit, the twenty-four-year-old Marcel Duchamp. One or two dealers such as Paul Guillaume were showing an interest in Negro sculpture; the poet Apollinaire became an art critic for *L'Intransigeant* and Arnold Schoenberg's atonal music was attracting startled attention in musical circles. Events and innovations such as these, which were taking place in other European countries as well, were in the process of profoundly changing the course of art history, but while they were wildly exciting to those in advanced cultural circles they had not yet penetrated broader levels of art practice and appreciation. The products of the new experimental spirit did not constitute the "new art" that Carr had envisioned, nor would she have been attracted to them. She had the opportunity to see some of the advanced work while she was in Paris, but she makes no mention of it. Her experience in Paris was not, as one might have imagined, that of a person responding with curiosity and elation to being in the great world centre of art or, like other Canadian artists, connecting at some level with the professional or bohemian student art community.

This somewhat reticent artist did, however, find her own level and her own connection. By the time she arrived earlier modernist innovations had already been going through the normal process of transmission, diffusion, modification and finally absorption into studio training and painting practice and had reached at least a degree of critical acceptance. Beneath the layer of daring innovation there existed a stylistic mode which could perhaps be considered a generic Post-Impressionism. Any number of variations were to be found and together they represented the absorbed and successive innovations of the Impressionists, the Post-Impressionist directions set by Gauguin, Cézanne and Van Gogh, and the Fauves, whose intense colour and violent brushwork had pretty well freed their art from representational intent.

This was the "new art" that Carr had come to see whether she knew it in advance or not; it was what found her. The chief agent of her introduction was a "very modern" English artist living and working in Paris to whom she had been given a letter of introduction by a friend in Victoria, Henry Phelan Gibb. According to her recollection of her first visit to his studio, some of his paintings pleased, others shocked. "There was rich, delicious juiciness in his colour, interplay between warm and cool tones [he knew the painting of Cézanne]. He intensified vividness by the use of complementary color. . . . [his] landscapes and still life delighted me—brilliant, luscious, clean. Against the distortions of his nudes I felt revolt."[10] On his advice she enrolled in classes at the famous Académie Colarossi where an instructor told her she was doing well and had good colour sense. However, she found the atmosphere of the classes stuffy, as she had previously found those in London's Westminster School. More often than not she could find no one to translate the French instruction for her. Fortunately Gibb's second recommendation was more profitable: that she leave Colarossi's and study under a Scottish-born painter, John Duncan Fergusson, where language would be no problem. Fergusson was three years younger than the now thirty-nine-year-old Carr, and he had received a certain amount of recognition in France as well as in England. Like Gibb a member of the Salon d'Automne, and accustomed to the French system of studio training and salon exhibitions, he was one of the "colorists" who had broken with an older generation of academic Scottish painters and were looking to Matisse and the Fauves for their clues. His work—at that time mostly portraits and figure studies—must have struck Carr with its bold new vision. But after only a few weeks in his class, illness, which seemed to dog her in big cities, forced her to leave the studio where he was teaching. She had been in Paris from October of 1910 to some time in December. The remainder of her stay in France would be spent in village locations where countryside and simple country folk were far more congenial to her temperament.

Following a trip to Sweden to recover from her illness—where she was pleasantly reminded of Canada and where there were family friends though apparently no art connections—she returned to France in the spring of 1911. Gibb was giving a class in landscape painting in the little canal town of Crécy-en-Brie, not far from Paris, and she joined him there. She had obviously made the sympathetic contact with him lacking which she found real criticism or instruction impossible to take, and he was a good teacher for her. Even if, as she noted, he frequently felt compelled to make allowances for her as a woman painter, he recognized her seriousness and determination. His wife was familiar with the kind of modern art to which Carr was being introduced and her explanations of its theoretical side were also helpful. Crécy was situated in the gently domesticated countryside of the Barbizon painters who had initiated plein-air landscape painting in France about eighty years earlier. A number of small oil paintings of the town with its tree-lined canal, balanced between painterly and descriptive intent, cool and greyed in colour, indicate that she was making progress towards "fresh seeing."

In June of 1911 Carr, still enjoying and needing the instructive proximity of her mentor, followed the Gibbs to Brittany where they were spending the summer. She stayed in the small village of St. Efflam, pursuing her own rigorous outdoor work routine, finding in the village church, the thick-walled houses or peasant kitchen interiors an invitation to realize the sensory meaning of rich colour applied in flat painty areas; or in the fields and woods of neighbouring farmlands and countryside the energizing poten-tial of direct bright brush strokes of pigment. The Brittany paint-ings such as BRITTANY, FRANCE speak vividly of a startling change in her painting outlook and style. Although modest in size and complexity they indicate clearly that she had arrived at an understanding of picture-making quite new to her, and one which placed her in the central stream of twentieth-century art. She now grasped a fundamental principle of modern art which involved the distinction between the forms and objects that the eye sees out there in natural space and the different "sense" or meaning that shapes have when they respond to the flatness of the picture plane. It was a matter for the artist (and the spectator) of seeing and thinking first of all in terms of coloured pigment rather than real objects in nature. The pictorial means of realizing the new way of seeing were common to Post-Impressionist prac-tice: using a palette of light-filled colour applied in direct touches unblended on the canvas surface; employing a system of contrast based on hue rather than tone (giving colour to shadows); assigning value to negative spaces; paying attention to flat pat-tern; eliminating detail. Carr made what was for her a radical shift with astonishing rapidity and impressive authority, creating her own kind of colour shorthand for translating what she saw in nature into direct slabs or patches of colour or brush strokes that

MENDING THE SAIL 1911
Watercolour, 25.7 x 30.8 cm
Private collection

were often vigorous and directional in their handling. What she saw was treated as coloured sensation rather than as the conveyor of information or deep feeling, though the energy and vibrancy of the work corresponded to her mood of excited discovery—the discovery of the expressive possibilities of paint itself. Later on she would uncover a deeper level of experience from which she would be able to work.

Up to that time, apart from the early "school" pieces of San Francisco or the paintings done in England, Carr had painted in watercolour. In France she moved to oil, the medium of the "new art," its coloured density suiting it naturally to the kind of perceptual vision she now shared. But she also painted in watercolour, employing two distinct styles. There are scenes of village streets or squares with their stone buildings and trees and village folk chatting or busy about their tasks; an outlining brush gives these watercolours a graphic quality and sometimes they seem like tinted illustrations. Possibly they were painted in St. Efflam, for they are quite different from watercolours unquestionably painted in Concarneau, a fishing village on the southern Brittany coast. She spent six weeks there in the fall of 1911 working with the New Zealand painter Frances Hodgkins who had been living and working in France since 1908.[11] Carr's paintings in that medium, produced during her last few weeks in France, are marked by a pictorial sophistication and vigour that immediately distinguish them from those she had done not so long previously in British Columbia. There are figure studies and sparkling boat scenes and interiors with women mending sails or going about other everyday tasks. Concern for detail is gone, main forms are blocked in with a sure direct wash or drawn with a heavy brush; figures are grasped as compositional units to be marshalled according to pictorial needs—brought dramatically forward into the picture plane, moved right, left, up or down, or cut off by the margin. Highlights and shadows become part of an overall tonal structure rather than the means of representing the subject with convincing volume and depth.

Before she left France in November Carr had two of her paintings accepted for the 1911 Salon d'Automne, Paris' annual large open, and juried, exhibition. The strong patterning, the loose and light-filled touches of brilliant colour, the arbitrary crimson

VANCOUVER STREET 1912 or early 1913
Oil on cardboard, 18.4 x 22.9 cm
Private collection

tracery of trees and fields in BRITTANY LANDSCAPE, one of her
two entries, show clearly her sources in the Fauve paintings of
Matisse, Marquet, Vlaminck, Derain and their colleagues, even
though their liberating message came to her filtered through the
mediation of Gibb and others.[12] To be hung in a big Paris show
was significant for Carr, though in the broader perspective it
carried with it limited distinction since, while it included such
already important names as Matisse, Bonnard and Léger, it also
included hundreds of others as little known as hers, and probably
in some cases less accomplished.

That event, however, can be taken to symbolize her gradu-
ation, in terms of her own progress, into the mainstream of
modern art. She had been in France altogether fourteen months,
much of it spent ill or out of the country or moving around. Still,
she had produced a body of small but vigorous, assured and
sophisticated paintings demonstrating a sensuousness and awareness of pictorial form that would be part of her artist's equipment
from now on. Most important, she had shaken off old-world
shackles and joined the ranks of modern painters. The next major
step would involve connecting her new artistic position with her
roots in British Columbia and Canada; but unfortunately that
step was to be delayed for fifteen years.

Loss of Momentum

The small painting VANCOUVER STREET of 1912 or early 1913 is
an example of Carr's work after her return to Vancouver from
France, her new-found taste for brilliant arbitrary colour and
vigorous spontaneous brushwork at first undiminished in the
West Coast environment. Sales of paintings and returns from
teaching, however, were not sufficient to support her, and she
made the decision to return to Victoria. Whatever its limitations,
that city would be her home and place of work from now on. A
large exhibition of her work, which she herself had mounted for
public showing in Vancouver in April of 1913, did not bring her
the practical or critical rewards she had hoped for, and she
claimed to have been "rejected" by Vancouver because of her
new style of painting. The fact is, of course, that neither Vancouver nor Victoria had the power to grant other than the most
limited and parochial support—critically or financially—much as

she would have welcomed unequivocal moral support from any direction. She might have been encouraged had she known that her work, as art historian Dennis Reid has pointed out, was in advance of most Canadian painting at this time.[13]

During the next fifteen years Carr did not entirely stop painting as she claimed,[14] though the sharply diminished activity in comparison with her previous furious output might have made it seem so to her. She had built a small three-apartment building (Hill House) on the lot that came to her from her father's estate, expecting that the rental income would enable her to live and continue to paint in the rooms and attic she kept for herself. As matters turned out, painting was put aside while she acted as manager, landlady, caretaker and troubleshooter for her tenants. (She later turned the tribulations of these painful years to literary advantage in her book *The House of All Sorts*.) To supplement her income she engaged in a range of activities, raising bobtail sheep-dogs for sale as well as "small fruit, hens and rabbits," and hooking rugs and making pottery with Indian designs. She did manage to paint a little and in the mid-twenties she resumed a public stance as an artist by exhibiting in annual shows organized by local or regional societies, particularly with the Island Arts and Crafts Society (both watercolours and oils) in 1913, 1916, 1924 and 1926. In 1926 she had a one-person exhibition in conjunction with Victoria's annual fair and she also showed with the Seattle Fine Arts Society in 1924 where one of her submissions won an award. Some of her entries in those exhibitions were produced prior to 1913—Indian subjects or work done in France—but titles like UPLANDS, IN THE PARK, AUTUMN WOODS, THE BIG PINE, THE POINT, ARBUTUS TREE, ESQUIMALT indicate that she some-times escaped from the demands of running the apartment house to paint from nature. In the 1920s, as her financial situation eased, the escapes became more frequent and of slightly longer duration. Still, compared to her earlier work and her later compulsively prolific output, her production during this fifteen-year span was not enough to indicate a sense of urgency or direction. Art had ceased to be the preoccupying centre of her life. The revealing words in Carr's statement "I never painted now—had neither time nor wanting. . . for about fifteen years I did not paint" are "not wanting."[15] She had not yet found the inner centre for her art, yet once the appropriate signals were given she snapped out of her artistic apathy almost overnight.

A Climactic "Sea-Change"

In 1927, at the age of fifty-six, Carr might perhaps have been expected to continue working and exhibiting within the limited though gradually expanding parameters of the regional scene, her art following its own pattern of slow evolution out of her French experience, or slowly petering out as she advanced in age. However, in the sense of full and assured productive maturity—of becoming fully "Carr" in her art—her career was just about to begin. Her preparatory period spread over nearly forty years, but an event triggered by forces and people she knew little or nothing about and lasting only a few weeks, had the effect of catapulting her into full, committed productivity which would lead her within a year to a mature and commanding style.

The event came about as a result of paintings of West Coast Indian subjects which Carr, working in the isolation of her British Columbian island unknown to her eastern Canadian painting colleagues, had been producing between 1907 and 1913. During her years as a landlady she came to the attention of several people who were connected with influential eastern Canadian institutions and who immediately recognized her individuality. One of these was the ethnologist Dr. C. Marius Barbeau, who had been employed by the Geological Survey of Canada and later by the National Museum in Ottawa and had been studying the native peoples of British Columbia's Skeena and Nass river valleys. Between 1911 and 1929 he made a number of trips to that area, collecting poles and other artefacts for his own and other museums' collections, and heard from his Indian interpreter about Carr and a trip she had made in 1912 to the Skeena valley. He was interested enough to tell Eric Brown, the director of the National Gallery in Ottawa, about her, and to visit her in her studio where on several occasions he bought her paintings and hooked rugs.

Another of those who actively collected artefacts for museums at the time was Victoria's Dr. C. F. Newcombe, a physician by training and an experienced ethnologist and naturalist by vocation. He too became Carr's friend, purchasing a number of her paintings and supporting her in various ways. His son William Arnold—the indispensable "Willie" of her book *Hundreds and Thousands*—later became her handyman who helped around the house and in the moving and crating of her paintings. A constant supporter and collector of her work, as well as a close friend, he eventually became a trustee of her estate. Today the Newcombe Collection, made up of works he and his father acquired from her, is in the Provincial Archives in Victoria where it forms one of the major public collections of her art.

There was also at this time Harold Mortimer Lamb, whose interest in Carr stemmed, unlike that of those previously mentioned, from his enthusiasm for art not anthropology. An English-born mining executive he was also a talented amateur art photographer, a friend of the New York photographer Alfred Stieglitz, and an art lover of informed and fairly advanced tastes. In Montreal, where he had lived before settling in Vancouver, he had come to know eastern artists who were part of a much more advanced art scene and were in general more sophisticated than those in the West. He wrote articles and reviews on art and artists for journals and newspapers, voicing among other opinions his strong advocacy of the Group of Seven painters of Ontario who were at that time drawing abusive comments from conservative critics. Once on the West Coast he wrote letters to the eastern art establishment protesting its neglect and ignorance of western artists, and became a valuable vocal presence in the local art scene. It was Sophie Pemberton, an earlier painting colleague of Carr in Victoria, who told Lamb about her, and in 1921 he wrote Eric Brown recommending that the National Gallery purchase Carr's collection of native paintings. Brown was not in a position at that time to respond positively and, not having seen her work, replied that he felt it was probably more appropriate to the purposes of the Museum than those of the Gallery, and no follow-up took place.

However, Brown and Barbeau were planning an exhibition for the fall of 1927 which clearly called for Carr's participation. Entitled "Canadian West Coast Art, Native and Modern," its purpose was "to mingle for the first time the art work of the Canadian West Coast tribes with that of our more sophisticated artists." The "modern" section included, along with Carr, the

American Langdon Kihn and Canadian painters Walter J. Phillips, Edwin Holgate, A. Y. Jackson, Anne Savage, Pegi Nicol and the sculptor Florence Wyle, all of whom had made brief trips to West Coast native settlements following Barbeau's lead. Carr alone of the group had made a sustained study of her subject and she was the best represented by twenty-six oil paintings as well as by some of her rugs and pottery with Indian designs. The exhibition opened on 30 November under the joint sponsorship of the National Gallery and the National Museum of Canada and was subsequently shown in Toronto and Montreal. Some watercolours sent in the shipment were not included in that show but were hung in the National Gallery's Annual Canadian Exhibition of 1928 from which the Gallery purchased three.

Carr realized that the context was ethnic rather than artistic. Nonetheless, the concept of the exhibition was unusual for its time, and for Carr it provided the opportunity to have her work hung alongside that of known and respected artists in a venue far removed from her habitual regional situation, the first such occasion since the 1911 Salon d'Automne exhibition in Paris. Even more important, it was the occasion through which she came to meet members of the Group of Seven, Toronto artists who were already well known as representatives of the most advanced art in English Canada, and to see their work—events that were to mark the most dramatic turning point in her career and to signal the full blossoming of her art.

She had been given a Canadian National Railway pass to eastern Canada to attend the exhibition opening and she allowed herself several days in Toronto in advance to meet members of the Group. On her way east she had met one of them, Frederick H. Varley, in Vancouver where he had been brought to teach at the new Vancouver School of Decorative and Applied Arts; later she would meet Franklin Carmichael and A. J. Casson. But now Arthur Lismer, A. Y. Jackson, J. E. H. MacDonald and Lawren Harris received her in their studios in Toronto. Those four and Varley had become the solid continuing core of the Group, and she was able to see Harris, who would become a major figure in her evolution, twice more on that trip.

The impact of the Group of Seven and their work was pivotal to Carr in three ways: the first was psychological, a question of morale; the second and perhaps most important was ideological —the goals and purposes they declared for their art set Carr in the direction she had been waiting to find, and their discourse gave her the words she needed to affirm and articulate her own intention. The third was the evidence of their paintings which in boldness of patterning and colouration were inspiring models of conviction and strength. The almost immediate effect of that trip on Carr was to put her back into full, excited painting activity. She tells us that three days after her return she was painting again and soon, with "sketch sack on shoulder, dog at heel, I went into the woods singing. . . . household tasks shrivelled as the importance of my painting swelled."[16] In March of 1928 she wrote Eric Brown that she was using gallons of paint and lots of canvas and was thrilled to be working at the Indian stuff again. From now on only failing health would interrupt the flow of her painting energy.

The lift to Carr's morale was to a considerable degree a personal gift from the Toronto artists who, sensing her insecurity and timidity, welcomed her with warmth and unmistakable sincerity as a painting colleague. Those who saw her work in the exhibition recognized her quality and her seriousness as matching their own. "Will they know *what's in me* by these old Indian paintings," she had asked herself anxiously before the Group had seen her pictures, knowing her potential was not yet realized.[17] She very much needed their acceptance of her as a person and an artist. And so, in response to one of her self-belittling remarks, Harris's words "You are one of us," echoing the mood of the week's various meetings with her, must have struck to her heart. For the first time she felt herself connected to a close community of important Canadian artists whose shared vision heightened their impressiveness as individuals and excited her as nothing had previously done. Back on the West Coast during the long years ahead, the sense of belonging to the serious art community of Canada would be stretched thin at times, but never again would the sense of isolation be crippling nor would she suffer the loss of spirit that had retarded her art for nearly fifteen years.

The ideology of the Group of Seven had been well articulated by the time Carr encountered them and it was to give her a renewed sense of purpose and fresh focus for her own art.

Although the Group exhibited as a unit for the first time in 1920 and showed as a group until 1931 (when it replaced itself with the broader-based Canadian Group of Painters), the work by which it is commonly identified was produced between 1913 and the early 1920s. By the beginning of the second decade of the century several Canadian painters with shared attitudes and concerns— most of them with a common background in commercial design—had come together in Toronto, then as now the lively centre of art activity in English-speaking Canada. (A. Y. Jackson had joined them from Montreal in 1913.) They believed that the European-derived styles and conventions of painting then prevalent in eastern Canada, including various modifications of impressionistic naturalism and of the Barbizon and Hague schools, were inadequate to deal with either the material or spiritual reality of Canada. In January 1913 two of the future central members of the Group. J. E. H. MacDonald and Lawren Harris, saw the "Exhibition of Contemporary Scandinavian Art" then showing in Buffalo, New York. As A. Y. Jackson later admitted, that exhibition was vitally formative for the future Group, as formative as Carr's meeting with them was to be for her.[18] There MacDonald and Harris found that thoughts and ambitions similar to their own had been given stunning expression in landscape paintings of northern European countries which bore much resemblance to Canada. That brief but galvanizing encounter affirmed their emerging ideological goals and offered painting approaches from which they could learn—although, of course, the Canadians were to develop their own individual styles and a shared group spirit. Almost at once the "new Canadian painting" began, the excitement drawing in one member after another. It proceeded on two assumptions: it would be an art of landscape; and the kind of landscape best suited to embody the spirit of a young and vigorous country would be the rugged wilderness of Canada's northland, with its awesome grandeur of lakes and forests and rivers, its open sweep of sky, or nature's impenetrable tangle—the kind of country farthest removed from the history and humanity-drenched countrysides of England and Central Europe. In the painting styles that developed, a close observation of nature fused with a sense for large, bold pattern which was both distilled from the scene and imposed as a felt design. That combination had been employed by the Scandinavian painters, and its lesson was further enriched by the influence of elegant art nouveau design with which all the members of the Group were acquainted. In general, paint was applied thickly, brushwork was direct and form-shaping, and brilliant colour made no concessions to atmospheric effect. In the late twenties, as members of the Group developed individually, they would venture beyond the untamed terrain of northern Ontario, with which they were first identified, in their quest for other types of nature symbolic of Canada's vastness. But their early work, which became inseparable from the popular rhetoric that developed around it, dominated painting for several generations in English-speaking Canada.

3   The Formation of a Mature Style

Following her momentous trip to eastern Canada at the end of
1927, Carr not only positioned her painting once again at the
centre of her life but she also began, apparently overnight, to
work in a style very different from that of her painterly Post-
Impressionist paintings of the past fifteen years. The painting
between 1928 and 1931 is the most conceptual and designed of her
career and, like her Fauvist-derived painting, the most strongly
marked by outside influence. This was the period of radical turn-
about: the period of her closest association with Lawren Harris
and his strongest influence on her thought and art; of Mark
Tobey's equally crucial impact and of contact with the larger
world of art through books and a brief trip to New York.

Critical Influences: Harris and Tobey

Whereas the Group of Seven's general stance of militant nationalism and their sense of great purpose were an important inspiration to Carr, their painting, however much it impressed her with
its boldness and largeness of feeling, had little direct effect on her
own. Lawren Harris's was the exception. The Harris paintings,
seen by her in the Art Gallery of Toronto in a room along with
those of other members, "are *alone*," she said. "Sometimes when
you enter the gallery the others die—they are a different time a
different place, a different world and there is always that dignity

and spirituality. . . . "[1] Again, "I have never felt anything like the power of those canvases. They seem to have called to me from some other world, sort of an answer to a great longing."[2]

By the time Carr met them most of the members had moved on from their earlier styles of closer Group activity. Varley in Vancouver was now inspired by the mystical potential of West Coast sea, mountains and moisture-laden atmosphere. Lismer had painted canvases of great faceted mountains; Jackson's work had taken on the dominant rolling rhythm that became his hallmark. Harris had abandoned the flatness, the heavy impasto and the decorative elements of his earlier painting and was moving towards a more metaphysical art as his ties to Theosophy became stronger. The locations for his paintings became more remote and austere, more humanless and preternaturally calm— bare trees, frozen lakes, mountains, glaciers—and his form assumed an appropriate equivalence: reduced colour range with increasing emphasis on the non-sensory blues and greens relating to distant space; suppression of detail or surface interruption in favour of smoothly delineated and modelled (and idealized) forms; light pervading the space of the picture or formalized into directional shafts, either device implying a symbolic presence. These were the paintings that struck Carr so forcibly, not the "very old ones [despite their] lovely colour" that Harris also brought out to show her.[3] His ABOVE LAKE SUPERIOR of 1922— an icon in the popular history of Canadian art—moved her deeply as did his mountain paintings of several years later. She subsequently described a sea painting,[4] which she saw in his house, in such detail as to leave no doubt that it had imprinted itself in her mind's eye: "A heavenly light lay upon one corner, shining peacefully. Three cloud forms, almost straight shafts with light on their tips, pointed to it. Across a blue-green sky, a long, queer cloud lay lower down, almost on the horizon, but you could move in and on and beyond it. A small purplish round island, then four long, simple rock forms, purple-brown, with the blue sea lapping them. Two warmer green earth forms and some quiet grey forms that might be tree trunks in the foreground. Peace. My spirit entered the quiet spaces of the picture."[5]

Harris's belief in painting as the reflection of metaphysical-spiritual states of being was to have great influence on Carr over the next couple of years, and though his stringent and icy path to transcendence was not one she cared to follow, his pictorial principle of simplified forms in space as a means of achieving a desired expression was one she readily accepted. Within a few months she had given up the concern for painterly surface employed since her return from France and had started to translate what she saw in nature into three-dimensional pictorial forms, placed in depth-space and thus optically detached from the canvas surface. It was not Harris's deep and infinite space, however, that she adopted, one which he achieved through the hard-edge profile of his forms in contrast with their surround. Her method was to paint by "passage," adjusting the tonal contour of her forms so as to weave them into a cohesive spatial matrix. In this she was following in the steps of Cézanne who, in the words of Elie Faure, "forsook the sinuousness of profile for the magnificence of contour." There is a small irony in noting that Carr, who was such a champion of "modern art," in abandoning her French Post-Impressionist connection for a symbolic approach opted for one of the less generative currents in the great mix of modernist art. The fact of course is that the term "modern art" for her meant in a non-specific way art that was against tradition and not naturalistic in intention like that with which she had grown up.

Early and tentative stylistic changes reflecting the impact of the Harris paintings she had seen in Toronto in late 1927 can be noted in two modest undated canvases that must have been done in early 1928 before the advent of Mark Tobey in her life. SKIDEGATE and THE CRYING TOTEM (Tanoo), relate to her 1912 paintings in their small format and in their handling of background as a decorative backdrop. The inscription "Skidegate" on the face of the former also belongs to her earlier practice of geographically identifying her subject's location in the interests of documentary authenticity, one which her symbolic intention would not require in the future. But compared to any of her 1912 paintings, the change in approach is striking; the tachist handling has disappeared, the surface is smooth, the forms are simplified and the muted colour now belongs to the depicted forms and not to the touches of pigment. The leafless vertical tree spars and simplified background trees in both are very reminiscent of Harris, as is the horizontally striated sky of SKIDEGATE.

SKIDEGATE 1928
Oil on canvas, 61.5 x 46.4 cm
Vancouver Art Gallery 42.3.48

While the impact of the eastern Canadian artists was still strongly with her, and Harris's mentoring through the channel of correspondence had begun, Carr experienced another short but vital encounter, this time with the American Mark Tobey. Almost twenty years Carr's junior, Tobey had come by way of New York and Chicago to teach in the small, progressive Cornish School of the Arts in Seattle. Carr had a number of acquaintances in Seattle, occasional visitors to Victoria in the 1920s who rented rooms from her. It was they who tried to coax her out of her landlady doldrums and who encouraged her participation in the Seattle exhibitions she entered from 1924 onwards. They included the artists Viola and Ambrose Patterson and Dr. Erna Gunther, an anthropologist well known in the field of Northwest Coast Indian culture. Tobey became part of their circle and he too spent a week in her studio in the early twenties. He was most likely the artist who advised her that her beds, dishes and meals would wait, "young morning on Beacon Hill won't. Don't tether yourself to a dishpan, woman! Beds, vegetables! They are not the essentials."[6]

In September of 1928 Tobey came to Victoria and gave a three-week "advanced course" in Carr's studio. Despite the difference in their ages, they had some things in common. Both were religious by nature and placed high value on the spiritual life. His association was with the eastern mysticism of the Baha'i faith and—a few years following Carr's contact with him—with Zen; both beliefs were vital in the development of his mature art. While on the West Coast he became an avid admirer and collector of Northwest Coast poles and other native artefacts. He had seen the famous Armory Exhibition in New York in 1913 and, like Carr, had spent time in Paris. But the avant garde art when first available to them had left both of them untouched, and, as it happened, both arrived late at their respective artistic maturities.

An energetic man of enquiring mind, open to ideas and an eager experimenter, Tobey came to Carr's studio to teach some time before the various elements of his art and his thinking had coalesced into the style by which he is known. At his exhibition in 1929 in New York "realistic paintings... hung beside undulating abstractions, and still life beside bizarre fantasies."[7] He was, according to Viola Patterson, an authoritarian teacher, forcing on his students whatever ideas had captured him at the time. But this did not prevent his being an effective and forceful instructor, and Carr, who apart from the debt to Harris, which she always freely acknowledged, was disinclined to discuss her sources of help or influence, was enthusiastic about him. In a letter to Eric Brown she described him as " a man that interests me very much, very modern and very keen. . . . I think he is one of the best teachers I know of. He gave a short course of classes here in my studio, and I felt I got a tremendous lot of help from his criticisms. He was very keen on my summer's work [the results of her trip to northern Indian sites] and his crits, I feel, will be very useful in the working out of many problems connected with my summer's work which I hope to do this winter."[8]

He stayed in her studio once again in the spring of 1930 while she was visiting in Toronto and New York, and in November of that year, in obvious acknowledgement of his earlier helpfulness to her, she sent him five dollars to come and give her a criticism. He did not come, though he sent her a letter with advice which she records in her Journals. She should, he said, "pep my work up and get off the monotone, even exaggerate light and shade, to watch rhythmic relations and reversals of detail, to make my canvases two thirds half-tone, one third black and white. Well, it sounds good but it's rather painting to recipe, isn't it? I know I am in a monotone. My forests are too monotonous. I must pep them up with higher contrasts. But what is it all without soul? It's dead. It's the hole you put the thing into, the space that wraps it round, and the God in the thing that counts above everything. Still, he's right too. I must pep up."[9] Perhaps a vigorous oil-on-paper sketch of a dark forest interior with its flashes of white and black (VAG 42.3.56) reflect that advice. In any case, Tobey's comments reveal the very specific pictorial nature of the criticism she received from him. Much of Harris's advice tended to moral encouragement: "to work from [your] own considerable strength"; "not to be influenced by anyone or anything"; "to accept the necessary artist's rhythm of alternating despair and elation"; to "disregard the critics." His pictorial advice tended to be general: "to strengthen [your] design"; to "follow a first canvas by another of the same subject so that the idea will unfold"; and in any case, it was all distanced through correspondence.

Nearly thirty years later, in 1957, Colin Graham, who as Director of the Art Gallery of Greater Victoria had kept in touch with Tobey, described the American artist's struggles with Carr. "He [Tobey] had evolved a system of volumetric analysis of forms combined with what he called the pressure of light areas against dark and vice versa. The latter he had derived from the work of El Greco while the former, as I understand it, was a form of analytical cubism. He described Emily as still heavily entrenched behind the buttresses of Impressionism and its off-shoots and it was only after prolonged resistance that she came to him one day and said 'you win.'"[10] Tobey similarly recalls his "battle with her to teach her form as I knew it relative to the principles used by El Greco, Rembrandt and all those associated with the conventions relating to Leonardo's discoveries."[11]

When visiting Victoria in 1957 Tobey was to claim credit for Carr's acquiring an authoritative style. "She could not have developed to conceive the great swirling canvases, the wonderful tree forms, unless there had been someone to indicate the way for her. I was that someone."[12] That the three-week teaching presence of Tobey was important to Carr is certain, and the unresolved nature of his work at the time makes it equally evident that his influence was not through his own painting but through discussion and criticism relating specifically to pictorial form. His mystical leanings did not preclude an ability to give practical painter's advice with the conviction she needed in a time of uncertainty. The kind of forceful and prescriptive role he played was fraught with risk to friendship in Carr's case, for, as he later recalled after fighting some point in his instruction that he was driving home and to which she eventually gave in, she also finally turned against him "with a fury" that he did not understand.[13] Harris could never have played that role, and indeed she once admitted, at a time when she had outgrown her dependence on him, that in criticism he "is too kindly, doesn't smack hard enough to be stimulating."[14]

In retrospect, what might appear to have been an extravagant claim to influence on Tobey's part has to be accepted in its essence; it was Harris who inspired Carr and reactivated her drive, but it was largely Tobey who showed her how to translate that inspiration into painted form. A comparison of the two early

KITWANCOOL TOTEMS d.1928
Oil on canvas, 105.4 x 68.3 cm
Hart House, University of Toronto

MOVING FORMS 1930 by Mark Tobey
Watercolour and gouache, 27.4 x 49.9 cm
Seattle Art Museum 36.41

WESTERN FOREST 1929–30 (top)
Oil on canvas, 128.3 x 91 cm
Art Gallery of Ontario, Toronto

KITWANCOOL 1928 (left)
Oil on canvas, 101.3 x 83.2 cm
Glenbow Museum, Calgary

Untitled (forest interior) 1928
Oil on unstretched canvas, 52.1 x 48.5 cm
British Columbia Archives, PDP 931

Untitled (formalized trees
and foreshore) 1929 (top)
Charcoal drawing, 47.9 x 62.2 cm
Vancouver Art Gallery 42.3.134

INSIDE A FOREST II 1929–30
Oil on canvas, 109.9 x 69.8 cm
Art Gallery of Ontario
Bequest of Charles S. Band

1928 paintings cited above with KITWANCOOL TOTEMS, which was perhaps started before Tobey's arrival that fall but certainly was finished under his instruction, shows a striking difference in authority and handling. The entire concept is assertively sculptural in a manner new to Carr, and the modelling of the poles in particular fulfils like a prescription Tobey's "system of volumetric analysis of forms combined with. . . the pressure of light areas against dark and vice versa."[15] Further to Tobey's credit perhaps, a keen sense for the strategic placement of light and dark areas in her compositions remained with her to the end. And possibly too, as he claimed, he made some contribution to the "great swirling canvases" even though they appeared several years following his teaching session in her studio; perhaps his vitalistic view of the world contributed to the swirling expansive component in her work which would soon become its animating character. It is also quite likely that the gains were not all on Carr's side; the ropey abstracted trees in Tobey's 1930 canvas MOVING FORMS have a striking affinity with some of her handling of nature forms in canvases such as WESTERN FOREST, which he could have seen in her solo exhibition in Seattle that year, or others when he stayed in her studio that spring.

Tobey is usually credited with the introduction of the particular structuralized element in Carr's work that marks her style after his visit until it disappears in 1931 and that has been variously referred to as "Cubo-Futurist,"[16] "cubo–expressionistic"[17] or the author's own "cubist-derived."[18] This stylistic innovation appears as suddenly and as strikingly foreign to her previous work as Post-Impressionism had been sixteen years previously. The "futurist" connection is readily seen in KITWANCOOL where a strong dynamism carves terrain and sky alike into curved or diagonally slanting spears, bars and slices. Painted in 1928, before she had full mastery of the new painting ideas that Tobey was hurling at her, it is a peculiarly unresolved canvas in which the poles—theoretically what the picture is about—neither share in the dramatic pictorial life of their setting nor have the strength to hold that setting in effective contrast. Carr's early struggle with the proto-cubist idea can be seen as she applied it to forest imagery in several studentlike canvas studies of forest interiors. The idea has fully developed in canvases such as INDIAN CHURCH

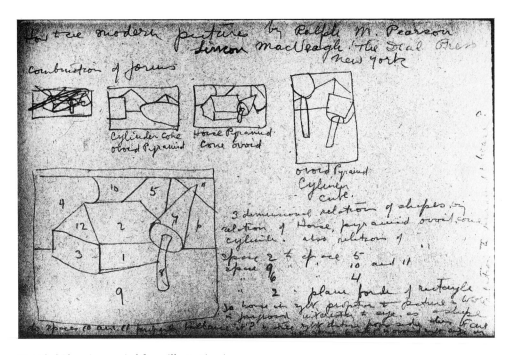

Untitled (drawing copied from illustration in
Ralph Pearson, *How to Look at Modern Pictures*) 1928
Graphite drawing, 15.2 x 22.9 cm
British Columbia Archives, PDP 5733

of 1929 or in several large charcoal drawings (Vancouver Art Gallery collection) where entire trees or their complicated foliage are carved and chiselled into a micro-structure of geometric forms, curving, overlapping, zigzagging. In other versions, such as INSIDE A FOREST II, the forms are more continuous and fluid. If we are to look for the theoretical progenitors of Carr's "cubism," we should think back to the "sculptural cubism" of Fernand Léger in his paintings of 1909, or to the 1912 cubist paintings of Kasimir Malevich. Beyond that, of course, we go to Cézanne from whose structurizing principle the whole cubist idea with its enormous ramifications for the subsequent history of modern art took off. Carr herself was never interested in the theoretical side of Cubism nor did she make of cubist structurizing a concept of form for its own sake; she remained firmly rooted, so to speak, with her trees. Her "cubism" was solid and single point of view; structurizing is what she was about.

Although it is the use that Carr made of a cubist idiom that is relevant to her art, the fact that it came to her in Victoria through Tobey is also interesting. In an attempt to understand Cubism he had formulated his own model by imagining the path of a fly as it moved in a contained compartment of space from one object to another, "generating a complex of line, and by its many crossings, imaginary planes and shapes. Although related to the objects in the room, this secondary matrix of form was independent of them, and was entirely the product of movement."[19] A "cubist" canvas that Tobey painted of Carr's studio in 1928 is often cited to substantiate the cubist connection between them, though its discontinuity of space and fragmentation of natural forms is quite unlike Carr's sculptural and spatially consistent approach; nor does the painting seem to exemplify Tobey's own theory. That she took note of his canvas, however, is indicated by several fairly straightforward sketchbook drawings she made of the paraphernalia in her studio not too long after his stay.

Other Influences
A book by Ralph Pearson, *How to See Modern Pictures*,[20] helps to account for the appearance of the cubist element (or one might say the structural turnaround) in Carr's work. It was used by Tobey in his Victoria teaching sessions,[21] and evidently became a

support medium for her when after three short weeks of instruction she was left on her own to work out his principles. The repeated heavy pencil markings in her own well-thumbed copy in the British Columbia Archives, dated September 1928 in the flyleaf, the time of Tobey's stay, testify to its value for her. Its message of design, of simplification, of elimination of detail as characteristics relating to one or another kind of cubist-derived modernism was pervasive in books of the twenties. Those ideas have long since been absorbed into the history of the beaux-arts tradition, but they were in their time the currency of advanced teaching and appreciation theory, and Carr had several other examples in her own collection though the Pearson was probably the most consistently useful to her. The reproductions in books and magazines were then as now a major channel for the transmission of art ideas to artists working away from main centres. For Carr, whose moments of actual contact with major advanced art were few and usually brief, and whose need was for words as well as for reproduction models, books with their ready reference were vital.

Didactic and somewhat simplistic to modern readers, Pearson's book was very much in a stream of thinking current in art theory and training at the time, and in its combination of practical pictorial analysis along with an assertion of art's deep expressive values it was an answer to her needs. Numerous diagrams with arrows and lines connecting strategic points in a given composition accompany his discussions of form relationships in picture making, all part of the emphasis he placed on design "which the modern movement had rediscovered. . . as one of the most essential qualities which determines a work of art." Following Cézanne's route, he points out that all forms in nature can be reduced to primary geometric solids so that "a mountain is a cone or pyramid, a tree top is a cube, sphere, or ovoid, its trunk a cylinder,"[22] and so on, a necessary process of abstraction in the artist's search for "inner realities." Distinguishing between two design approaches, he enlists the cubists to clarify his point: in the first approach, design is considered paramount to all else, justifying any extreme of distortion or conventionalization to achieve its goal—a route which may lead, as it did with the cubists, to partial or complete abstraction. While granting the cubists their great liberating contribution to twentieth-century art, Pearson clearly represents the second approach which "uses only as much abstraction as necessary to achieve universalisation." In a long footnote heavily emphasized by Carr's pencil, the value assigned to Cubism is that of having simplified the problem of apprehending design.[23] It is the structuring principle *underlying* Cubism, the emphasis on design, that he—and Carr—are after. A series of sketches from one of her drawing books shows her, like a student, following his advice: a cube, cylinder and cone with their volumes shaded in, followed by drawings of cubic "lay" figures, and finally a totemic carved figure cubically analyzed. In another sketchbook she has faithfully copied one of Pearson's diagramatic analyses of houses, trees, hills and other landscape forms into cones, cylinders, cubes and so on.

Pearson's advice continued that given by Tobey (using the same book) and reinforced the general counsel Carr was receiving from Harris by correspondence. In a letter to her, undated but probably from the fall of 1929, Harris stressed the importance of design to her: "You can in one sense, in one part of you, forget the spirit... it is innate in you—but push the forms to the limit in volume, plasticity, and precision and relationships in one unified, functioning greater form which is the picture. .... the last picture you sent me shows a greater concern for precision of design but the form could be intensified, given even more power."[24]

Pearson's book reveals its relevance to the direction she was taking in other ways. "Static and Dynamic Symmetry" is the title of one of its chapters, "dynamic symmetry" being then a prevalent catchword in art teaching and discussion, a credit to the popularity of a book of that title by Jay Hambidge from which Pearson draws his argument (and a copy of which was also in Carr's possession). A reproduction of a work by the German-American Arnold Feininger, a semi-abstract composition of exaggerated dynamic qualities, demonstrates Pearson's discussion of the diagonal and the perpendicular to the diagonal. A work by Pearson himself, a "picture in which cypress trees have been reduced to their simplest elements and woven into design" bears the grid Carr pencilled over it as she sought to trace out its "dynamics" and drive home his instructions.[25] Other reproductions—the small, poor black-and-white prints of the time—

TREE TRUNK 1931
Oil on canvas, 129.1 x 56.3 cm
Vancouver Art Gallery, 42.3.2

represented other variations of modes of simplification and abstraction being investigated as the cubist-futurist idea spread. In addition to the Feininger, there was, for example, a work by Charles Sheeler (showing a ship whose motion is suggested by abstracted sails seen as overlapping and intersecting curved planes) that invites comparison with Carr's handling of forest forms in canvases of 1929 and 1930. And there are a number of works by artists whose names history has forgotten, all examples in which "design has been imposed on reluctant material."[26]

The reproductions in another of Carr's reference books, one that she had from the end of 1930, raises tantalizing analogies to certain of her works dating from that time. *The New Art* by Horace Shipp, published in 1922, is a "Study of the Principles of non-representational Art and their application in the work of Lawrence Atkinson," an artist who had a brief connection with the English vorticists. A number of his monolithic stone or wood sculptures, referred to as "abstractions" and bearing titles such as "Adastral" and "The Eternal," bear a family likeness to some of Carr's tree forms involving repeated overlapping profiles, as in the single trunk of TREE [TRUNK] of 1931.

Such books serve to remind us that by the time of Tobey's contact with Carr, Cubism and its direct offspring in many European countries (Futurism, Orphism, Cubo-Futurism, Vorticism and other "isms") had been absorbed into the more general move towards abstraction which it had triggered. A generic style based on various kinds of structuring and geometric forms of simplification (somewhat as Post-Impressionism had also become a generic mode available for Carr's adaptation sixteen years earlier) was pervasive in the practice and teaching theory of art at the time—a style which in the thirties and forties in Canada the art-uninitiated would identify as "modernistic." Although there was little if any art with even the appearance of cubist-based modernism being produced in her immediate environment in 1928 or 1929 to have set her on her way, there were artists in other parts of Canada whose work would at least have been supportive to the stylistic moves she was making. One name that comes to mind is Bertram Brooker. Carr would have just missed his solo showing at the Toronto Arts and Letters Club in January 1927, on her trip to eastern Canada, but she could well have seen some of his work, for he was a close friend of Lawren Harris and strongly influenced by the latter's views of spirituality in art. His symbolic abstractions of the years 1927–30 employ smoothly modelled and defined forms in space, frequently illuminated by dramatically directed light shafts, and their spiritual intent, declared in such titles as ENDLESS DAWN, THE DAWN, THE DAWN OF MAN, would also have appealed to her. Brooker included a reproduction of one of Carr's paintings in the 1929 edition of *Yearbook of the Arts in Canada* of which he was the editor.

There was to be one further, and again brief, interface with the larger world of art when in April 1930, at Harris's suggestion, she extended her Toronto trip to visit friends on Long Island and then spent a week in New York. Her round of gallery visits was greatly facilitated when Arthur Lismer, whom she ran into unexpectedly, invited her along on his tour of the spring shows. Unfortunately, her diaries do not cover her New York visit, though in *Growing Pains* she mentions having seen works by Kandinsky, Braque, Duchamp, Arthur Dove (whose exhibition at Alfred Stieglitz's gallery An American Place closed on 22 April), Archipenko, Picasso "and many others." While there it would have been possible for her to see an exhibition of Charles Burchfield's watercolours, and she does record a meeting with Georgia O'Keeffe in Stieglitz's gallery where she saw and liked some of her work. Marcel Duchamp's NUDE DESCENDING THE STAIR was decidedly among the works in "those modern exhibitions [that were] a wonderment beyond my comprehension, but they were certainly not beyond my interest. In some of them I found great beauty which stirred me, others left me completely cold; in fact some seemed silly, as though someone was trying to force himself to do something out of the ordinary."[27]

Within a few hours of her train's departure for Toronto she managed a visit with Kathleen Dreier to whom Harris had given her an introduction. A sophisticated and knowledgeable enthusiast of modern art and a writer, lecturer and organizer of exhibitions devoted to its dissemination, she was co-founder, along with Duchamp, of the Société Anonyme. She and Harris had become friends through one of the Société's exhibitions, the "International Exhibition of Modern Art," a portion of which was shown in Toronto in the spring of 1927. Carr had a brief but

rewarding discussion with Dreier about abstraction and abstrac-
tionists and saw some of the paintings from her extensive collection of modern art. It is particularly interesting that Carr made
note in her recollection of a painting by Franz Marc,[28] for she herself had already painted a few shadowy forest interiors penetrated
by shafts of faceted light, pictures that seemed to contain echoes
of the lyrical, pantheistic Marc of the years 1911–13. One of
these paintings was hanging in a Group of Seven exhibition in
Toronto at that very time.[29] One wonders whether the Marc she
saw in Dreier's apartment struck her with a sense of something
strange and new and yet well-known? She also left New York
with a copy of Dreier's book *Western Art and the New Era,* which
she digested over the next few years and which doubtless played a
part in confirming and adding to the ideas about art and life
already received from other sources.

The New York trip was important for Carr in giving substance
to some of the advanced art that she had not had eyes to see when
she was in Paris and had since encountered only in books or
through discussions with Harris, Tobey and perhaps others.
Although she was not in need of a total recharge of battery and
start-up, as she had been in 1927, it was helpful now to be able to
see and challenge or confirm herself in that broader context—far
broader than the Canadian context the Group of Seven had provided for her. What direct influence the experience had on her
painting is impossible to say with any certainty. She was at the
time of her visit still working on formally structured paintings of
dark and claustrophobic mood without much hint of the freer
open world she was about to enter. Did the looser, freer painting
of Burchfield or the primal organic forms of Dove open up a
vision of a more fluent painting of her own?

These few years of formal paintings were enormously concentrated ones in which Carr, making up for much lost time, came
through a series of powerful influences with her own vision
formed and consolidated. When she moves into the freedom of
her late nature paintings, students can leave behind their anxiety
to track influences, for they will have been absorbed into the
expression of a vision so intensely held and so commensurate
with the dimensions of her whole being that she will find all her
sources within herself.

4 An Interior Evolution: Belief and Attitudes

The personal forces that drive artists to make art—and to make the kind of art they do—are many and complex, quite apart from the larger cultural conditions within which they must work and which are prior determinants of the range and nature of their expression. Carr's early attraction to a vocation whose true nature she could not have foreseen had to do with the simple and intense satisfactions of the natural painter exercising her given, and then trained, skills to make images of familiar things she loved. While it was acceptable for the wives and daughters of colonial Victorians to be casual painters of landscape and flowers, the seriousness of her commitment to art was a declaration of independence. The sheer intensity of her passion indeed isolated her from the conventional atmosphere of Victoria. As she became ambitious for her art, it was that it should be good, that it should "matter," and the response that she constantly required from the simplest to the most critical level of acknowledgement was not for the sake of praise or reputation but for the affirmation of her work's worth. By the time she reached her maturity and began realizing her considerable potential, the earlier obvious impulses had been absorbed, and drives until then inchoate had been clarified: her ambition had come to relate to deeply spiritual aspirations and ideas which in the best of her art are fused with her medium. Her ultimate philosophical equation was a triad that encompassed God, art and nature. We touch her thought through her art, but if we are to appreciate its full dimension and the way in which her art and her spiritual convictions were melded, we should make some attempt to understand her ideas and how they developed.

For many of the great artists of Carr's time, a belief in painting as an end in itself—an aesthetic pursuit with self-defining goals— was a sufficiently powerful motivation to produce some of the most significant work of the twentieth century. Carr's art belongs to a contrary strain in modernism, one that looks for its sustenance in spiritual sources, a strain so counter to the domi- nant aestheticism of the late 1930s and forties that, as Maurice Tuchman has pointed out, to use the word "spiritual" could be harmful to an artist's career.[1] Understandably, Carr, whose spiri- tuality was firmly rooted in her temperament and her upbringing, was unaware that the simple reaching-for-God which directed her art and her life might be part of such a larger strain.

In *Hundreds and Thousands* Carr wrote: "To church-goers I am an outsider, but I *am* religious and I always have been."[2] Carr grew up in a Protestant family circle where religion provided authority for moral behaviour, and its practice loomed large in everyday life. There were regular morning prayers and Bible readings at home, frequent visits by one sister's missionary acquaintances and Sunday School classes organized by another sister. Sunday itself was a day set aside for special rituals. Although she rebelled against the "large, furious helps" in which religion was served up at home and resented the "prim, orthodox, religious" posture of her older sisters,[3] long after she was freed of family authority she continued church-going herself, never affiliating with any denomination but always looking for the experience that would lift her out of the realm of mundane existence.

There was space out in the open for the God who "got so stuffy squeezed up in church," out there where "he was like a great breathing among the trees. . . . he just *was*, and filled all the uni- verse."[4] That adult statement reflects the mature person, con- scious and secure in her belief; but even as a child her intimate experiences of nature—the smell, the look, the touch, the feeling—were capable of transporting her into realms of bliss, experiences that were from the beginning part of an innately religious nature that also needed some kind of church ritual for fulfilment. Probably that innate religious trait affected all the moves and decisions contributing to her ultimate artistic expression, even though the first conscious link between her art and religion was not forged until November 1927 during her momentous first meeting with Lawren Harris and the Group of Seven circle. That date also marks the beginning of the published Journals in which she writes at some length about her spiritual life and its relation to art, and of the decisive change in direction and quality that her life and art were taking. The Group, in providing her with the basic philosophical-spiritual construct in which her mature painting would be grounded, was crucial to her resurgence.

Some of the Group members were more philosophically inclined than others, but all were familiar with the writings of the American transcendentalist Ralph Waldo Emerson and his followers Walt Whitman and Henry David Thoreau. The transcendental acceptance of an ideal spiritual reality beyond the world of ordinary experience, which intuition can grasp and which infuses all things, underlay the Group's belief structure and the place of art within it. Its members were also strongly spiritual in their orientation, and while individuals followed their own particular persuasions, all assumed the interconnectedness of art and religion. Bertram Brooker, a prominent Canadian artist of the day, quoted Whitman in his editor's introduction to the 1928–29 *Yearbook of the Arts in Canada*, a quotation which would have been endorsed by all members of the Group: "The attitude of literature and poetry [we can extrapolate 'poetry' to refer to all art] has always been religious and always will be. . . . the religious tone, the consciousness of mystery, the recognition of the future, of the unknown, of Deity over and under all, and of the divine purpose, are never absent but indirectly give tone to all."[5]

Frederick Housser had already written the story of the Group in *A Canadian Art Movement* published in 1926, a story (in his telling of it) more inclined to edification than to information. He, along with his painter wife Bess (later to become the second Mrs. Harris), was a close friend and associate of the Group and a theosophist who identified with and helped formulate their ideology. Crusading and rhapsodic in tone, Housser's book conveys the shared excitement of the painters as they pursue their vision of an intensely nationalist art based on a realization of the psychic potential of their great land. In it he observes "that when the soul of a man and the soul of his people and environment meet, the creative genius of a race bursts into flame. . . . the message that the Group of Seven art movement gives to this age is the message that here in the North has arisen a young nation with faith in its own creative genius."[6] He makes it clear that the "Canadian consciousness" which is central to the Group's belief has nothing to do with the "political consciousness" of common nationalist thinking.[7]

Carr was fresh from reading Housser's book when she met him and the Group in Toronto and saw some of the paintings that gave witness to their shared feelings. Both by temperament and through this medium, she was tuned in advance to respond to their message. And despite the differences in age, background and experience, there were already certain underlying parallels between Carr's attitude and practice and those of the Group. She too had found the old-world attitudes and painting conventions of her environment inadequate to express her Canadian West Coast experience and had looked for alternatives. In pursuing her Indian work she had, like the Group, sought out subject material that was indigenous to Canada and eccentric in relation to the painting around her; like them she had made her way to off-beat uninhabited corners of the country in a spirit of adventure and discovery. In fact, she had unknowingly followed Housser's dictum that the artist must "divest himself of the velvet coat for the outfit of the bushwacker and prospector."[8] She retained a deep bond with nature, perhaps deeper than some of theirs, for hers went back to her most intense childhood experiences; with her, nature would become broadly enough imagined to include the Indian fact. She was by temperament intuitive and spontaneous, even if intuition and spontaneity had not yet been theorized as part of her life values. And—most importantly—she too, though not committed to any orthodoxy, was deeply religious in her own way, the spiritual dimension being a condition of her existence.

On first seeing the work of these eastern Canadian artists she was rapturous: "If I could pray, if I knew where to find a god to pray to, I would pray, 'God bless the Group of Seven,'" a statement suggesting she had not yet found a belief to answer her adult needs. She felt at once that she might find God in their work—"the God I've longed and hunted for and failed to find."[9]

Carr was neither an intellectual nor a theorist, but she needed a few verities with which to form her personal rock of faith, and she needed to have them stated simply in language that she could interpret, adapt and develop in her own earthy and innocent way. They would be echoed, fortified and reified in many other things she read, saw or heard in the early thirties, for the Group was not formed in a cultural vacuum; but she recognized them first as *her* truths through the Group. They showed the equation even though she was already familiar with the terms: *God* (whether her term or some less charged 'universal life force'); *Nature* (the realm of things not created by man and which our own unaided senses can know); and *Art*, whose purpose it was to reveal the presence of the former in the latter. Through their talk and writing and painting the Group postulated an art in which spiritual and moral purpose was invested and one therefore worthy of man's highest aspirations—a concept to which Carr could harness her considerable artistic and spiritual drives and that could activate her unrealized strengths.

Harris and Housser among others within the Group's circle were theosophists, and theosophical principles transposed to a specifically Canadian consciousness played a large part in the Group's thinking. For instance, in the passage from Housser's book quoted above are two ideas supported by theosophical belief: that the rugged and austere North—specifically the northern part of North America—would play a special role in achieving the synthesis of nations, religions and sects which Theosophy held as a goal; and that only through knowledge of a particular, in this case Canadian, environment could the larger spirituality beyond be reached.

Lawren Harris was the acknowledged leader of the Group and the most philosophically and mystically inclined, a man whose warm and jovial surface manner did not always at first suggest the thoughtful and intensely spiritual person within. As a youth his prominent Toronto family had sent him to study in Germany where he encountered the anti-materialist thinking of the German romantic and symbolist movements and where his interest in comparative religions was awakened. Back in Toronto, having turned to painting, he became interested in Theosophy whose otherworldly emphasis and view of the artist's role in expressing the spiritual inner life was also attracting other artists similarly disillusioned with the dehumanizing effects of the industrial revolution. In 1923 he became a member of the Theosophical Society, writing articles for the *Canadian Theosophist* and other publications in which he presented views about Canadian art as interpreted in the light of theosophical doctrine.

Among the Group Harris was the most outgoing and generous-spirited to Carr and the one who appealed to her most as person and as artist. On visiting his studio in Toronto for the second time, she was convinced that "his religion, whatever it is, and his painting are one and the same."[10] Returning home to Victoria she found that his pictures were still vividly in her mind. "They have got there to stay. . . . They make my thoughts and life better. The memory of them is a never failing joy. They are the biggest strongest part of my whole trip East. It is as if a door had opened, a door into unknown tranquil spaces. . . . To me it's a clearer language than the others are using. Why, I wonder? I have never studied theosophy and such things and I don't think I want to. But there's something that gets at me, and if it is theosophy that gives that something I'd like to hear about it. It could be nothing bad that inspired those pictures."[11] Harris became her supporter and friend, and between 1928 and 1934 they carried on an intense correspondence, the first real "talk" she had had about the things that mattered to her most.

Harris's paintings, which spoke so strongly to Carr at that time, could indeed be thought of as expressions fulfilling theosophic principles. Their emphasis on light as a primary means of expression related to the clear white light of theosophic symbolism representing eternal truth prior to its splitting into self-asserting colours. Harris found his subjects in the inaccessible north of the North American continent, a part of the world from which some theosophists (particularly Helena P. Blavatsky, leader and founder of the Theosophical Society) anticipated a flow of spiritual energy. He painted from the forms that were specific to his own experience and country, but he stressed their abstract simplified form rather than their surface incident in the interests of the universal spirit that suffused them, an approach consistent with theosophical thought.

At Harris's suggestion, Carr purchased a copy of the Russian Peter Ouspensky's *Tertium Organum*, a text valued by theosophists which, after its publication in 1911, became for several decades an influence among European and American artists and theorists who sought solutions through adherence to mystical-occult belief systems. It is a highly theoretical treatise describing four stages of spiritual development corresponding to an ability to perceive four spatial dimensions—a book miscalculated to tell her the secrets she sought to find in Theosophy. Reading it on the return trip to Victoria she admitted that "I get glints here and there but such lots of it I don't understand. That's not strange since I haven't studied along these lines before. . . . I shall stick at it and try to see it in time for I am sure somehow it will help my work. It produces the quality of spaciousness in Mr. Harris's pictures that I lack."[12]

At some point Bess Housser sent her a book by Mme. Blavatsky (probably *A Key to Theosophy*, a simple question-and-answer book that Harris had recommended in a 1931 letter). And so Carr began a struggle to come to grips with theosophical doctrine. Theosophy is not a religion but rather a "synthesis of science, religion and philosophy" (the subtitle of Blavatsky's 1888 publication *Secret Doctrine*), which draws on occult and spiritual traditions of East and West, and on various concepts of evolution. Carr found it difficult to reconcile its teachings with her long-established Christian beliefs and she had helpful discussions with Harris on two visits to Toronto as well as with the Houssers. In the fall of 1933, after the last visit, she persuaded herself that "they [chiefly Lawren, Bess and Fred] escape into a bigger realm and lose themselves in the divine whole. To make God personal is to make him little, finite, not infinite. I want the big God."[13] But finally the esoteric theoretical nature of Theosophy proved irreconcilable with her own life experience. Her religious requirement included a "real God, not the distant, mechanical, theosophical one,"[14] a personal God to whom she could pray and who would speak to her. The presence of a personal God runs through the Journals like a supra-human father who is always there, divine but real.

And so Carr decided to go her own way. After attending a series of lectures by Raja Singh, A Christian Hindu and associate of Mahatma Ghandi, whose "child-like, simple faith—no sect, no creed, no bonds, but just God and Christ"[15] touched her deeply, she wrote to Harris in December 1933 telling him she could not swallow some of the theosophy ideas; and in January 1934 she wrote again, "snapping the theosophy bond." It was, she said, reading Mme. Blavatsky's book that did it; "her intolerance and particularly her attitude to Christianity. Theosophists say that one of their objects is study of comparative religions and on top of that claim theosophy is the *only* way. It's that pedantic know-it-allness that irritates me."[16]

Luckily she was able to find that even though she couldn't follow all the theosophy formula, "the substance is the same as my less complicated beliefs; God in all. Always looking for the face of God, always listening for the voice of God in Nature. Nature is God revealing himself, expressing his wonders and his love. Nature clothed in God's beauty of holiness."[17] She was afraid that she might have ended the sustaining association she had enjoyed with Harris and others in eastern Canada, in which support for her art and help in her spiritual quest had been so intertwined. Doubtless this fear kept her struggling with Theosophy for so long. She need not have worried that Harris would end the friendship because of her return to Christianity, but the vital period of their relationship was over, chiefly because her own strength and confidence had increased her independence.

Nonetheless, Harris's letters were crucial to her for their moral and emotional support, and since in them he responded to her questionings and encouraged her with simplified extensions of various doctrines; and with his artistic and philosophic stances into which those doctrines had been assimilated, she did absorb some ideas that had theosophic underpinnings. Thus, in a letter written in the first year after their meeting, he puts forward a fundamental principle of Theosophy: the need to get beyond one's personality which is merely the "locale of endless struggle, the scene of the wax and wane of forces far greater than itself," and notes that "the creative imagination is only creative and only

imaginative when it transcends the personal."[18] Again, several
years later on the same point: "The soul has a different life from
the personality—a deeper stream of consciousness—closer to the
immortal—it alone is affected by beauty, nobility and the deeper
more enduring motifs of men and the spirit that informs nature"
whereas personalities exist on the surface of life.[19] She picked up
this thought many times, even after she broke with Theosophy.
"Instead of trying to force our personality on to our subject," she
wrote in *Hundreds and Thousands*, "we should be quite quiet and
unassertive and let the subject swallow us and absorb us into it."[20]

In response to her uncertainty about her work and her posture
of modesty, which he may have felt needed shaking, he writes
that "the true artist is outside of social recognition. He puts himself (or herself) outside because he couldn't work otherwise. His
or her point of view is the opposite to the society attitude."[21]
Although Harris himself would shortly turn to abstraction, he
still held firmly to the belief common to the Group that the
artist's work should grow out of a prolonged attachment to a
place and an absorption of its underlying character—the very
"trees, skies, earth and rock *of our own place* (author's italics)[22]—
a central and frequently reiterated position of her own. These
and other general ideas regarding the attitude and the role of the
artist, which can be related to Theosophy but are not exclusive to
it, began to be echoed in Carr's own thoughts as she recorded
them in her writing or incorporated them in two public talks she
gave, one in 1930, another in 1935. Until 1928 we have no record
of Carr's ideas about art or religion[23] so it is difficult to tell
whether they were Harris's ideas absorbed and repeated or
whether they were her own which he had helped formulate.
There are, however, so many parallels on a simple non-
theoretical level between their beliefs, and the personal ties with
him were so strong at the time, that one concludes that much of
his thought—and through him that of the Group—became her
own.

One aspect of theosophic theory had a direct bearing on Carr's
art: the belief that nothing in life or nature happens by accident
but is part of a Divine Plan according to which natural forms
follow immutable rules of geometry and design. The writings of
Blavatsky assigned geometric forms their symbolic-religious

meanings which are laid out in charts and diagrams: the triangle, for example, was associated with the "universal triune godhead and the sides of the pyramid."[24] The belief that there was a superior spiritual reality existing behind or underneath appearances had practical consequences for the artist, for it implied an emphasis on design and on the abstract form underlying the surface accidents of nature. The constituent of abstract design was strong in Harris's paintings; he was advising Carr to strengthen that component in *her* work, and the period of their closest relationship was indeed the time of her highly designed canvases.

The view of life as a continuity, often referred to by Harris and a generative notion in Carr's mature painting, relates in Theosophy to a belief in Karma and reincarnation. The endless cycle of nature—youth, maturity, old age and decay—is a frequent theme throughout her nature paintings, which at this time she handles in a formal, designed way. In OLD AND NEW FOREST the different age groupings, composed of simplified tree forms which contain the energy within them, move in ranks from bottom to top and in depth by orderly overlapping planes parallel to that of the picture surface. Most of the canvases of these few years observe this basic form of orderliness: the alignment of major compositional components parallel to the picture plane. In INDIAN CHURCH, a painting which lends itself to interpretation according to theosophical principles and which Harris singled out for particular admiration, there is the frontal church façade and behind it the thick edge-to-edge backdrop. Even the more spatially dynamic FOREST, BRITISH COLUMBIA counters its diagonal recession with layers of strong frontal parallelism. Carr admits to this pictorial connection with the theosophists, if not with their doctrinal belief when, after "snapping the theosophic bond" with Harris in 1934, she says that she feels she is putting more into her paintings than she did "a year or so back when I was thinking design and pattern and painted more or less from memory of things I had seen. I am painting my own vision now, thinking of no one else's approach."[25]

Some of her strongest work belongs to this period, and yet all the time she was following Harris's advice and trying to "think design" the spontaneous in her was straining to emerge. "They" (the Easterners) were talking design while she was filling her

OLD AND NEW FOREST 1931–32
Oil on canvas, 112.2 x 69.8 cm
Vancouver Art Gallery, 42.3.23

INDIAN CHURCH (Friendly Cove) 1929
Oil on canvas, 108.6 x 68.9 cm
Art Gallery of Ontario, Toronto
Bequest of Charles S. Band

FOREST, BRITISH COLUMBIA 1931–32
Oil on canvas, 130 x 86.8 cm
Vancouver Art Gallery, 42.3.9

Journals with talk of God and the bursting, pulsing life in all growing things.[26] The enclosing and dimly lit darkness of these paintings on the one hand reflect her new perception of the natives' poles as carriers of subjective feelings of mystery and brooding, carried over into sympathetically expressive images of the forests. But may they not also reflect the tension—productive as it was—rising from her effort to follow the pictorial urgings of her friends with regards to design, and to see Theosophy as other than a "static frozen awfulness, sort of a cold storage for beautiful thoughts, no connect–up with God by Christ"?[27]

Carr never came close to a sympathetic identification with, or understanding of, theosophic belief. The fact is, of course, that she had made that long journey into its, for her, chilling atmosphere in the interest of her painting and in order to secure the continuing moral support of her eastern mentors. "There is such a lot of vague, queer, man–made rigamarole about the wheel of destiny etc. I got all churned up by the whizz of it. I admired Lawren's work so much. . . . I wanted to get a slant that would help me on my own so I listened and I thought and discussed with them," Carr was to say thinking back to those days.[28]

Still, however painful it had been ultimately worthwhile, for she came out of it with certain enduring attitudes towards her art and it forced her into an identification of her own basic earthy and joyful Christian God as the universal life principle immanent in all living things. Her temperament demanded that she discover such a spiritual connection if she were to engage her full painting capacity. From now on, though she would experience times of doubt and discouragement, she had found her direction and motivation and she was already painting the pictures.

Carr might not have been able to pinpoint the effects of Harris's philosophy on her own ideas and attitudes about art, but she frequently acknowledged his importance in her life in those early years of friendship when in his letters he opened to her "the rich cupboards of his heart, stored with art knowledge. . . riched with his own perception, his inner struggles, his bigness. . . his hopes and high aims."[29] His influence, channelling with it that of the Group, was pivotal in the formation of a philosophy that could empower her work. But there were several books in her personal library, either sympathetic to or themselves of transcendental persuasion whose heavy underlining indicates their use-fulness to her in enlarging and reinforcing those same messages. They all assume the central role of art in revealing the spiritual nature of the universe.

In the book *How to See Modern Pictures* by Ralph Pearson, a copy of which she had in her possession just as her correspond-ence with Harris was getting into full swing, we find the fol-lowing: "It is by expressing the felt *nature* of a thing then, that the artist becomes the mouth-piece of the universe of which he is a part and reveals to man, through 'the something plus' in a pic-ture, the nature as well as the appearance of the life and forms about him. This 'something plus' has to do with life. It is born of the artist's attempt to express the force underlying all things—the push of sap upward in spring, the heave and give of muscles, the urge of love to the fusion that means birth of new life, the pull of the love that protects age and infancy."[30]

Carr's lecture to the students and faculty of the Victoria Normal School in 1935 takes its title "Something Plus in a Work of Art" from Pearson and follows his line of thought for much of its substance. She is particularly attracted to the idea of the "felt *nature* of the thing" to be painted, the *sei do* principle Pearson had picked up from a theory of Japanese painting. In a lecture titled "Fresh Seeing," which she gave in March 1930 in conjunction with an exhibition of her work at the Crystal Gardens in Victoria, she stresses the principle of distortion which "raises the thing out of the ordinary seeing into a more spiritual sphere, the spirit dominating over the subject matter."[31] The source for this argu-ment is another book, *Painters of the Modern Mind* by Mary Cecil Allen, from which Carr made several pages of notes.[32]

She also had a copy of Katherine Dreier's *Western Art and the New Era: an Introduction to Modern Art* purchased at the time of her 1930 visit to New York when she met the author who was, like Harris, committed to theosophic belief. Dreier's book, a collec-tion of her crusading lectures in the cause of modern art, is based on a broad grasp of modern European and American movements that places the term "modern art" in a global context rather than in that of the Canadian consciousness, which was the Group of Seven's concern. Published in 1923, the modern art of her book's title comprised for Dreier the varied expressions of Cubism

(France and Spain), Expressionismus (Germany and Russia), Futurism (Italy), and Vorticism (England), and finally "Modern Art in America," which she describes as a "rather vague term as all these various movements came over to us at once."[33] She backs up an ecstatic discussion of Kandinsky—whose 1910 book *On the Spiritual in Art* was a key document for several generations of mystically inclined artists—by a rapid run through art history demonstrating that all art stems from the "great spiritual forces that continue to unfold and develop the spirit of man."[34] That and other general statements about art, such as the necessity to be true to one's inner nature while at the same time going beyond the merely personal, as well as the high moral tone and the frequency of catchwords and phrases intrinsic to transcendentally oriented dialogue at that time—soul, spirit, feeling, inner forces, spiritual expression and so on—would have had the same inspiring ring as Harris's words. They are, of course, the very words with which Carr's own writing is strewn.

Two notions of Dreier's may have struck Carr with particular resonance: the central importance of the imagination and the necessity of developing the senses, which are "the true guardians of the development of the soul,"[35] affirmed the sensory creative child in Carr. And Dreier's constant reiteration of "dynamic force" as the key to life and the new vision in art were words that certainly seemed to coincide with the more dynamic turn Carr's own art would soon take.

Housser had introduced Carr to the poetry of Walt Whitman and perhaps also to the writing of Emerson (a copy of whose essay "Nature" was among her books). Whitman's *Leaves of Grass* and other volumes of his poetry were daily reading and travel companions to the end of her life; they are referred to and quoted often in the Journals where their rhapsodic spirit drenches her own written feelings and thoughts. One can almost open the Journals' pages at random to get the sense of ecstatic life that nature evoked in her:

> The secrets are out. The bracken tips have unfurled and baby birds are squawking and flapping among the dense foliage. The trees are fully dressed, brilliant and 'spandy' in their new clothing put on with an imperceptible and silent push. There is nothing so strong as growing. Nothing can drown that force that splits rocks and

pavements and spreads over the fields. To meet and check it one must fight and sweat, but it is never conquered. Man may pattern it and change its variety and shape, but leave it for even a short time and off it goes back to its own, swamping and swallowing man's puny intentions. No killing nor stamping down can destroy it. Life is in the soil. Touch it with air and light and it bursts forth like a struck match. Nothing is dead, not even a corpse. It moves into the elements when the spirit has left it, but even to the spirit's leaving there is life, boundless life, resistless and marvellous, fresh and clean, God.[36]

Such passages echo the rolling and dithyrambic song of Whitman, his on-going reach for union with primal forces and with all of nature, the reach and the yearning that animated and found expression in her nature paintings.

Carr's view of the world and of the artist's role in it, which was reinforced in her reading, is seen to be most closely aligned with that of the American transcendentalists, whose attitudes she inherited through the Group of Seven, especially Harris. Trans-cendentalism, however, was only one drop in the larger pool of inward-turning philosophies and beliefs (including formalized creeds like Theosophy) that, since the turn of the turn of the century, had been attracting artists who were repelled by the dehumanizing materialism consequent on the industrial revolu-tion. Harris's personal search for the spiritual would lead him to abstraction, an artistic direction which, as in the case of his reli-gion, was too arcane for Carr to follow.[37]

Carr thus developed a spiritual tie to a host of artists most of whom she would not have heard of, others whose work she only briefly glimpsed in New York. Two were Arthur Dove and Georgia O'Keeffe, both of whose art absorbed influences from literature dealing with mysticism or the occult.[38] She would not have known of their spiritual inclination unless she recognized it in their work (as she had at once in Harris's). She felt it immedi-ately in William Blake's engravings at the Art Institute of Chi-cago which she went to see twice on her visit to that city in 1933.[39] And was there a glint of recognition when she saw work by Kandinsky, Dove and O'Keeffe in New York in 1930?

Carr's mystical intent—to express the oneness of the universe immanent in nature—can be recognized in her paintings because she was able to translate the intensity of her feelings into paint, something not all spiritually oriented artists are able to do. But it would not be there had she not clarified her vision through the language, as well as the work, of others. In the formulation of her simple set of beliefs, as in her art, she was able to take what she needed from the beliefs of others, remaining unaware of their historical, theoretical or doctrinaire substructures.

BLUNDEN HARBOUR 1931–32
Oil on canvas, 129.5 x 94.0 cm
National Gallery of Canada

5 The Indian Presence

During her youth Carr painted the conventional subjects of her time: still life, flower pieces, scenery, figure studies. For brief periods in the winters of 1931–32, 1938–39 and possibly early in 1941 she had a go at portraits. The splendid self-portrait showing her as a bespectacled sixty-seven-year old woman of stern mien wearing the loose, nondescript "uniform" she preferred in her mature years is the best of them. But she much preferred to paint trees. Once she found herself in her art she had really only two subjects—or rather, thematic sources—the Canadian West Coast Indian heritage and nature.

Images and echoes of the aboriginal culture of North America's Northwest Coast constitute a frequent and strong presence in Emily Carr's work. The Indian theme appeared early in her artistic career, and dominated the period of her great formal canvases; and though it largely disappeared from the work of her last ten years, when her attention turned to the exploration of nature themes, it resurfaced again in the final years of her painting life, having in fact, like a deep undercurrent, been there all the time. On the simplest level it can be seen merely as a continuing thread of subject matter, but it was a great deal more than that. It was part of her art's evolution and contributed to the deepening of her intent. Indeed the spirit that characterizes Carr's mature nature paintings—the sense of a unifying universal life force which animates the forests, woodlands, beaches and skies—to some degree at least developed out of her prolonged immersion in the native art and culture of her part of the world.

The Old Indian Culture

The culture of the aboriginal peoples of this continent's North-west coastal region is recognized today as one of the world's richest and most distinctive. Many products of its past greatness found their way into public or private collections scattered throughout the world before measures to protect them were taken by Canadian officialdom in belated recognition of their great heritage value; or, for that matter, before natives them-selves, awakening to the vanishing of their inheritance, began to reclaim of it what they could. The Northwest Coast native Indians' culture is undergoing a process of renewal these days, not only in response to external factors affecting all native cul-tures in today's world but also prompted by the resurging sense of identity and inner endurance that characterized their ancestors.

The days of the old tradition, of course, are gone forever. Its most vital period was reached in the nineteenth century when, after several thousand years of slow evolution, it was stimulated for a while by the arrival of white foreigners who, however intrusive, brought with them their trade opportunities and their tools and materials. Then were produced the monumental poles and other carvings with which the average white person identifies the culture, and which became the subjects of Carr's paintings. They were sacred forms, part of the larger ceremonial life of the Northwest Coast Indians, by which they asserted their cultural identity and their place in the cosmic order of things while ensuring its continuity through time. In their rich mythology the Indians' unity with the whole of nature and the universe was symbolized through significant animals who were their spirit ancestors, some of whom, featured as crest-animals, established the owners' hereditary claims. The mythology provided the characters—the creatures of land, sea and sky as well as some mythical beings—which the native artist carved into the pole where, by familiarity with long-established representational for-mulae, the native could readily identify them as bear, wolf, eagle or raven. To those not in possession of an iconographic key, these creatures in their carved forms on a pole appear as assemblages of somewhat generalized parts, compounds of human and animal attributes rather than clearly identifiable animals. It is an encoded art form in which the native's complex view of the universe is deeply imbedded—an intricately layered formal structure reflecting his dependence on his natural environment and his belief in the supernatural powers that invested it, a structure compounding beliefs and assumptions hidden to those outside the culture and even only dimly perceived by those who have made a study of it.

Even so, to the sensitive viewer the totemic forms have a powerful presence and carry a message that is more than merely aesthetic. A strong creature-ness asserts itself. One sees creatures piled on top of one another up the length of a cedar pole, squeezed within the tight confines of the vertical column, bound in timeless iconic immobility by ancient rules of formalization. One sees the preponderance of huge bulging eyes, tongues and great rows of teeth, of ears, of paws that hold and mouths frequently in the act of swallowing another creature. A message of strange and compelling power is there for anyone to read through the body's involuntary empathy with other creatures sharing the basic conditions of phenomenal being as well as states of fear, anxiety (the need to be "all eyes and ears"), restraint, and so on. We receive such messages from the rigid, restricted positions in which they find themselves, and from the stern, ungiving expressions that the artist has carved into them. The art speaks of a shadowy world of tension, where at times the forces of control and containment are barely able to hold the restless and daemonic spirits that are straining to get out. This dichotomy is also expressed in ceremonial practices of some of the northern tribes: the wild spirit of man that belongs to the dark forces of his universe and is tamed through ritual dance and ceremony. Curiously, Carr's own situation (and some of her painting) during the years 1928–30 suggests a parallel, a period when she is working within the constraints of "design" and Theosophy while her impulses to freer expression are awaiting liberation. The native's art equally embraces other moods when the spirits slumber and dream within their carved confinement, a state of mysterious quiescence which also finds its expression in her work.

TERRIBLE TOTEM, KOSKIMO 1930
Watercolour, 36.8 x 26.7 cm
British Columbia Archives, PDP 609

A Commitment

The native presence was a normal part of the Victoria environment of Carr's youth, enriching the repertoire of available subjects and motifs for her and other artists with a touch of local
exotica. Her early notebooks yield a number of tiny sketches in
competently handled watercolour of Indian canoes from nearby
reservations pulled up at water's edge or making their way across
the bay. A sympathy for the natives themselves soon added to the
appeal such subjects held for her. Her contempt for anything she
could interpret as pretension led her to gravitate towards people
in simple walks of life whose hold on basic human values was
uncomplicated by excessive cerebration or social airs. Because
natives lived outside the class of society whose narrow values she
had rejected early in life and in relation to which she considered
herself something of an "outsider," she felt a certain bond with
them. Sophie Frank, a native woman living on the North Vancouver reserve became her lifelong friend. She would usually
manage to find qualities of honesty and forthrightness in the
Indians she met on her trips and when she came to know the great
carvings of the northern natives, she thought of them in the context of the human beings who had produced them and who, she
felt, had carved their own admirable human qualities into them.
She did not regard the poles and carvings she painted as detached
art works from which lessons in aesthetic form might be learned.

Her first notably Indian work—direct drawings and watercolours—was done in 1899 on a trip to Ucluelet on the west coast
of Vancouver Island, then a remote reserve of the Nootka, as they
were known at that time. She and her older sister Lizzie went at
the invitation of a friend of the latter who taught at a Presbyterian
mission school and thought, correctly, that Emily might like to
sketch there. There is nothing remarkable about such competent
little paintings as CEDAR CANIM'S HOUSE, UCLUELET, B.C., done
by a woman of twenty-eight who had already studied art for several years in California. It is the choice of subject that holds a hint
for the future.

She speaks proudly of meeting an old chieftain during this trip
who, after staring intently into her eyes,[1] accepted her on her own
terms as a person, even though they had no words for communication, and she was delighted to have the villagers give her the

CEDAR CANIM'S HOUSE, UCLUELET 1899 (top)
Watercolour, 17.9 x 26.5 cm
British Columbia Archives, PDP 2158

TOTEM WALK AT SITKA 1907
Watercolour, 38.5 x 38.5 cm
Art Gallery of Greater Victoria. Private collection
Intended gift to the Art Gallery of Greater Victoria
Thomas Gardiner Keir bequest

Indian name Klee Wyck (laughing one).[2] Perhaps too on this trip
for the first time she made the conscious observation that was to
be important to her and to her art: that the natives had not broken
their long-standing bond with nature and knew themselves to be
but a part of its larger pattern of change and continuity.

Although Carr often sketched in the native settlements in Victoria or North Vancouver, she dates her conscious commitment
to the Indian theme from 1907, when she and her sister Alice
made a summer trip to Alaska where they visited Skagway and
Sitka. The latter, an American naval station by the time of their
visit, had originally been a Tlingit village and Russian trading
post, but there were still natives living there and some poles—not
Sitkan Tlingit but Kaigani Haida[3]—had been moved to form the
well-known "Totem Pole Walk." This was the first time she had
seen any of the fine monumental sculpture of the northern native
tribes and she would catch glimpses of more in the villages on the
return trip. She did some sketches in Sitka where they were seen
by an American artist, T. J. Richardson, who sold in New York
the work done during his summers in Alaska. He commented
that her drawings had true Indian flavour, and on the boat trip
back she did some thinking: "The Indian people and their art
touched me deeply. . . . By the time I reached home my mind was
made up. I was going to picture totem poles in their own village
settings, as complete a collection of them as I could."[4] As the next
four to five years were to show, this was a commitment she took
very seriously.

About sixty years earlier the Canadian artist Paul Kane had
produced a monumental record of Indian life from the Great
Lakes to the Pacific, and in British Columbia there had been the
occasional topographer or recording artist working with an
explorer's ship who painted an Indian subject. But no one—
certainly no woman—had undertaken a sustained investigation
such as she proposed for herself.

The larger Indian culture of British Columbia is made up of
seven major linguistic groups. The southerly tribes—those more
accessible to Carr—were the *Nootka* (now called the West Coast
people) of the northwest coast of Vancouver Island; the *southern
Kwakiutl* whose territory covered the northern part of the Island
and extended across the channel to the coastal mainland; and the

Salish of the lower mainland area. The northern grouping, usually considered a special subdivision by anthropologists, included
the *Haida* of the Queen Charlotte Islands, the *Tlingit* of the Gulf
of Alaska region, the *Tsimshian* of the Nass and Skeena rivers area
and the *northern Kwakiutl* (or Bella Bella) who lived in an area
south of the Tsimshian. Although their art came from a shared
cultural matrix, each tribal group developed distinguishing
stylistic and expressive characteristics. It was a broader cultural
territory than Carr probably realized, but she managed at least
to visit some part of each region once, and several a number
of times.

Carr was thirty-six at the time of her 1907 Alaskan trip. The
small paintings she was still doing following her time in England
pleased their audience when Carr showed them in Victoria's exhibiting venues and they made suitable gifts for families and
friends, but that did not constitute a purpose commensurate with
her ambition for her art. Up to this point, though well trained in
art according to her time, she had not found either any distinguished perception of the outside world or any deep content
within herself with which to empower her art. Creating a project
for herself—the making of a record of the villages in their native
settings—provided her with the moral and social purpose she
needed, and even though at first not primarily an artistic purpose,
it served as a bridge to carry her through to her mature work.
The trips to native sites, eight in all, which began in 1908 and
covered a period of twenty years, gave her the opportunity of
prolonged familiarity with the Indians' work. They resulted in a
varied and substantial body of work which did indeed record a
number of poles that had remained undocumented despite the
activity of early photographers; but much of what she did on
location has remained artistically valid as well, and together it
reveals the seriousness of her purpose and throws light on her
working methods. And it was the basis for the large number of
paintings on Indian subjects that she produced during her
lifetime.

1899–1927: Early Indian Work
The white invaders, whose tools and materials had stimulated
native artists to produce their most impressive work, had also

brought with them their diseases which drastically diminished tribal populations. At the same time, the progressive super-imposition of social practices, legal structures and religious beliefs onto those of Indians by government agents and missionaries were effectively ending the old ways of life in native communities. Naturally, deterioration was slower in more remote communities. As the culture lost its integrity, villages in accessible areas became fair game for the predators who began their activity around 1875, and by the 1920s, according to Douglas Cole, "as a result of private and museum acquisition, natural decay, and occasional wanton destruction, the British Columbia totem pole had become an endangered specimen.[5] The largest remaining clusters were at abandoned and isolated villages on the Charlottes, on the Nass and along the Skeena rivers, the last made accessible only by the wartime completion of the rail line from Edmonton to Prince Rupert."[6]

Even by the time Carr was making her early trips, many of the villages were deserted and in those that were inhabited, village life retained only echoes and memories of what it had been. Still, though the great poles were no longer being carved, many of them remained standing along with the impressive wooden houses which also had their important place in the culture's mythic structure. While in varying states of decay they still were situated in the natural settings—protected coves or inlets or river banks—which their original inhabitants with unerring wisdom had chosen for them.

Speaking of the trips later Carr remembered that "to reach the villages was difficult and accommodation a serious problem. I slept in tents, in roadmakers' toolsheds, in missions, and in Indian houses. I travelled in anything that floated in water or crawled over land."[7] Travelling conditions were never comfortable, especially to the more distant locations, but in her writing on the subject Carr exaggerates her isolation on the trips. There were usually missionaries or their friends to help, a railway or shipping representative to make connections for her and perhaps accompany her on portions of the trip. She herself was good at making contact with natives who could put her up and take her in a fishboat or other conveyance to her next destination. None of which diminishes the determination and courage involved for a

THE LONE WATCHER (Campbell River) d. 1909
Watercolour, 54.6 x 36.2 cm
Collection of David Gooding, Vancouver

ALERT BAY (incorrectly dated 1910) (right, above)
1909 or 1912
Watercolour, 76.7 x 55.3 cm
Vancouver Art Gallery, 42.3.109

HOUSE POST, TSATSISNUKOMI 1912 (right, below)
Watercolour over graphite, 55.4 x 76.6 cm
National Gallery of Canada

woman on her own and of her background in undertaking such
a program.

In the summers of 1908 and 1909 she visited coastal settlements
on northern Vancouver Island, particularly Alert Bay—the location of many drawings and paintings—and Campbell River. THE
LONE WATCHER, a 1909 watercolour of Campbell River, is one of
the many products of these first excursions from which canvases
were developed in 1912. The well-known studio watercolour
SCHOOLHOUSE, LYTTON in Montreal's McCord Museum,
though dated 1910, is more likely a record of a 1909 visit to several villages in the interior of the province—Lytton, Hope and
Yale—where there were no carvings but where she could enjoy
the ambience of village life. There are two watercolours in the
Vancouver Art Gallery collection of Alert Bay and Tsatsisnukomi, both dated 1910, which would indicate a trip to the Alert
Bay area that year, but a serious illness in the spring and her
departure for France in July suggest rather a slip in her dating.

Her experience in France gave her a fresh approach to picture-
making, but it did not diminish her determination to carry on
with her program of painting native poles, and in 1912 following
her return she made a first long and ambitious trip to northern
villages where she saw some of the fine native work done when
the traditional culture was at its height. (See Map A, page 228.)
Starting out in July from Vancouver, where she had once again
rented a studio, she proceeded north, stopping at southern
Kwakiutl villages on the eastern coast of Vancouver Island and on
the mainland coast across the Strait of Georgia. Fortunately, she
almost always inscribed the more substantial sketches from these
trips with the place names (often inventively spelled) and the date
as well, recording the places where she stopped and worked:
Alert Bay, Mimquimlees, Tsatsisnukomi, Karlukwees, Cape
Mudge and Gwayasdums. Two watercolours of paired interior
house posts were done in the Kwakiutl village of Tsatsisnukomi
while another, a studio watercolour done on her return, depicts
canoes drawn up on the beach in front of the same village's row
of houses. Her trip took her farther up the coast and then up the
difficult Skeena River to the cluster of villages scattered around
the mining town of Hazelton, the traditional territory of the
inland settlements of the Gitksan people. There she did a number

of sketches of the villages of Kitsegukla, Kispiox, Kitwanga and Hagwilget.

In August she set out for the Queen Charlotte Islands, the home of the Haida whose great seagoing war canoes, cedar long-houses and refined art forms have made them legendary. The Haida had suffered particularly in their contact with white people; a smallpox epidemic in the 1860s had so reduced their numbers that by 1915 there were fewer than six hundred remaining. All the villages except Skidegate and Masset, where the survivors of the epidemic had regrouped, were deserted by the end of the century, and there had been no totem-pole carving since the 1880s. Carr visited Skidegate and Masset and, except for Ninstints (today a world heritage site), the other main Haida locations, all accessible only by frequently rough sea. The abandoned villages of the Charlottes moved her intensely, the ghostly presences of the old carvings standing as silent witness to the life that had been—as her recollections in *Klee Wyck* tell us—Haina, Cumshewa, Skedans, Tanoo, Cha-atl, Yan and Ka-Yang. Watercolour sketches like SKEDANS IN THE RAIN demonstrate her natural painterly lyricism and show us what she saw, and sixteen years later a painting of the same subject would also convey the emotional flavour of her experiences. Altogether, the 1912 trip was a phenomenal success in terms of the quantity of work she was able to do, the relative wealth of fine Indian material that still remained, and the first impact of those northern villages which would never leave her.

The watercolours of 1912, done on the trip or from its material in the studio once she was back home, add to their veracity the pictorial assurance and something of the verve she had acquired in France. In CEDAR HOUSE STAIRCASE AND SUNBURST, a watercolour done in the Kwakiutl village of Mimquimlees on Village Island, the handling is direct and confident and the colour has a life of its own. In one of Tanoo, HAIDA TOTEMS, Q.C.I., three poles act as stable compositional units held in an ovoid of encircling art nouveau curves while sky cleanly cuts out the involuted profile of flat forest backdrop. The strong blues and yellow and touches of vermilion again recall the French experience. The lyrical CUMSHEWA with its elegant decorative foregound arabesques shows a similarly unmistakable art nouveau influence,

SKEDANS IN THE RAIN 1912
Watercolour, 55.9 x 76.5 cm
British Columbia Archives, PDP 2311

CEDAR HOUSE STAIRCASE AND SUNBURST (left)
(Mimquimlees) 1912
Watercolour, 69.2 x 54 cm
British Columbia Archives, PDP 2810

as do other studio watercolours of 1912.

Although one or two rather tentative oils of Indian subjects of earlier date exist, in 1912 for the first time she began developing the Indian sketches into canvases. In these Indian paintings we see her trying out variations of her newly acquired "modern" way of seeing and imposing them on the Indian material. There are several radiant canvases in which the breaking of light into little patches of coloured pigment emphasizes the impressionist legacy to Post-Impressionism, as in MAUDE ISLAND TOTEM. A group of narrowly vertical paintings deal with sections of single poles in which greyed opaque hues—grey blue, grey pink, grey green— flatten out the picture space, a flatness that is secured horizontally by strapping the space with decorative friezes of background foliage, fence and sky, and vertically with the truncated pole. SKIDEGATE is one such canvas in which she found a solution to the problem that totem poles presented to painters: how to deal with a thin needle shape whose figure-ground relationship shifts as it rises in the vision against a background of open space. In several medium-sized paintings she made use of the broad, flat Indian housefronts to help formalize the composition and shift emphasis to the picture plane, as in OLD VILLAGE OF GWAYAS- DUMS. From time to time a flavour of one of the Post- Impressionists from whom she indirectly drew—Gauguin, Cézanne—is suggested, as in a canvas ALERT BAY. Whether the colour is chalky and greyed or clear and brilliant, in general these Indian paintings of 1912 have a painterly immediacy like the paintings actually done in France, the result of her flaked brush stroke and the assertion of pigment and colour. These are studio paintings and in their decorative rhythms, the spreading of colour to the edges of flattened forms, the emphasizing of negative space, the heightened awareness of design they all show her new pictorial mastery. Several large canvases indicate the height of her ambition and confidence at this time: the sober (and probably unfinished) INDIAN HOUSE INTERIOR (Tsatsisnukomi), a brilliantly coloured painting of Yan and one of Tanoo dated 1913.

Some of these canvases must have been painted very shortly before April 1913, when she rented Drummond Hall in Vancouver and mounted a public showing of almost two hundred Indian pictures she had painted over the past fourteen years.

CUMSHEWA 1912
Watercolour with graphite and gouache
mounted on board, 55.8 x 75.4 cm
Collection of Alan G. Wilkinson, Toronto

HAIDA TOTEMS, Q.C.I. (Tanoo) 1912
Watercolour, 76.2 x 55.9 cm
Paul Kastel, Kastel Gallery, Montreal

MAUDE ISLAND TOTEM d.1912
Oil on cardboard, 58.7 x 30.8 cm
Private collection

SKIDEGATE (shark pole) d.1912 (below)
Oil on cardboard, 63.4 x 30 cm
Vancouver Art Gallery, 42.3.73

POTLATCH FIGURE (Mimquimlees) 1912
Oil on canvas, 44.5 x 59.7 cm
Dominion Gallery, Montreal

OLD VILLAGE OF GWAYASDUMS d.1912 (top)
Oil on cardboard, 66.4 x 96.9 cm
Vancouver Art Gallery, 42.3.52

THE WELCOME MAN (Karlukwees) d. 1913
Oil on card mounted on masonite,
95.3 x 64.8 cm
Private collection

ALERT BAY 1912
Oil on canvas, 61 x 92.3 cm
Private collection

VILLAGE OF YAN, Q.C.I. d. 1912 (bottom)
Oil on canvas, 98.4 x 151.8 cm
Private collection

Obviously wanting to understand the culture of which the art was an expression, as well as to educate her audience, she prepared a lengthy lecture "on totems." Having conscientiously read up on anthropological material,[8] she discussed the Indian social structure, ways of life and ritual and ceremonial activities, and distinguished between several kinds of carved poles. The talk then went on to describe her personal experiences of some of the villages she visited and problems and pleasures she encountered while sketching. Over and over she refers to the fine moral qualities of the native people—their honesty, their quiet dignity, their poetry—in comparison to the white people. Although she was always uncomfortable on public occasions, and certainly extremely nervous about speaking in public, she had invested a lot of hope and energy in her Indian work and she actually gave the lecture twice during the course of the showing. She ended her presentation with a statement of high moral purpose: "I glory in our wonderful west and I hope to leave behind me some of the relics of its first primitive greatness. These things should be to us Canadians what the ancient Briton's relics are to the English. Only a few years and they will be gone forever into silent nothingness and I would gather my collection together before they are forever past."[9]

The previous fall, Carr had approached the provincial government with a request that they purchase her collection of Indian paintings, a move which would have given public acknowledgement to her years of effort and financed further excursions to the northern Indian villages. To her great disappointment, the proposal was turned down on the advice of Dr. C. F. Newcombe (an amateur but knowledgeable anthropologist and a field collector for museums) whom the government had called in as a consultant. Although Newcombe admired her work, he saw that their brilliant colour and other painterly qualities detracted from their value as objective documents. Despite his negative report to the government, and despite his role as an agent for the raiding of the poles she loved (an activity she may not have understood), he became her friend, purchasing a number of her paintings and supporting her endeavours in other ways.

However unfortunate for Carr at the time, Newcombe's obser-

vation as far as the 1912–13 paintings are concerned was just. Her
conversion to a new vision in France had somewhat subverted her
original recording intention; her concerns had become more
painterly than documentary in focus. The paintings were therefore flawed from the Museum's point of view, and in truth they
were not invariably successful as paintings either. When a mode
of painting that relates to the perceptual aspect of vision, as in
some of her impressionistically painted works of this time, is
applied to a subject so inescapably loaded with acquired meanings
and overtones as native poles and villages, the result may be
incongruous—a misfit of subject and style. Carr's real difficulty,
though, was that the need to respect the identifying detail of a
pole's carved configuration ran counter to her newly found taste
for colour and Post-Impressionist brush work, dividing her
intention. This was not a problem when she was dealing with the
broad forms of native canoes, or with only a section of a pole seen
close up, or, of course, when she simply succumbed to the seduc-
tion of Fauve colour for its own glorious sake, as in the small brilliant painting ALERT BAY . But it was a problem she failed to
solve in several canvases where the poles' mass was small in relation to the large picture space and where she resorted to harsh
black outlining of detail in order to hang onto the poles' complex
iconography.

An awareness of the ambivalence of intent in her work at that
point no doubt was a factor in the sense of defeat that over-
whelmed Carr between 1913 and 1927, a period when she painted
a little from nature but produced no Indian work at all. To supplement her income during that difficult time she did, however,
make use of Indian designs, based on drawings she made from
pieces in Victoria's Provincial Museum and from books, in
hooked rugs (begun around 1915) and as decorations for small
pottery pieces that she began to make in the 1920s—ashtrays,
amulets, bowls. The pottery pieces were simple bisque-fired,
hand-formed and unglazed pieces, which sold well to Victoria's
summer tourists, and she continued making them until 1930. It
bothered her a little to think that she was exploiting the natives'
artistic property for commercial purposes, but she consoled herself that she was scrupulously faithful to the original designs. Her

ALERT BAY (with Welcome Figure) 1912
Oil on canvas, 65.1 x 47.9 cm
Private collection

serious interest in the Indian theme was far from exhausted, however, and she returned to it in 1928, after her critical trip to eastern
Canada, with fresh validation for her commitment.

1928–31: Renewed Purpose, New Approach

During the twenties a number of Canadian artists, sharing the
spirit of mounting nationalism which the Group of Seven had
initiated in painting, had gone to the western reaches of the
country, extending the vision of a vast and robust land. Among
many others who were becoming aware of the West as representing a part of Canada's character, and who were including
Indian art as part of that Canadian-ness, were A. Y. Jackson,
W. J. Phillips, Anne Savage and Edwin Holgate, all well-
established artists in eastern cultural circles. They, as well as the
earlier Paul Kane and the American Langdon Kihn, like Carr,
were included in the "Exhibition of Canadian West Coast Art,
Native and Modern" mounted jointly by the National Gallery
and the National Museum of Canada in Ottawa in the fall of
1927. That exhibition, in bringing together objects made by
native Indians along with work by contemporary white artists
who had used such material as subjects for their paintings, gave
institutional recognition to the growing perception of Indian
work as art. At the same time it confirmed Carr, who was gener-
ously represented in the show, in her long-standing commitment. The introductory remarks of both Marius Barbeau and
Eric Brown in the show's catalogue emphasized the significance
of Indian art, and Brown, who was a strong supporter of the
Group of Seven and had been well indoctrinated in their
ideology, stressed its Canadian-ness: "[The Indian's art] was at its
best as deeply rooted in his national consciousness as ever had
been our sense of traditional art and, in his weapons, architecture
and ornaments and utensils produced from the materials to his
hand, we can see how able and seriously he had held to them so
long as his national consciousness and independence remained."
Echoing their thoughts Carr herself said, in an article "Modern
and Indian Art of the West Coast" which appeared in the *Supplement to the McGill News* of June 1929, that "the Indians of the west
coast of Canada have an art that may be termed essentially
'Canadian' for in inspiration, production and material it is of

NASS RIVER POLE (Gitiks) 1928
Watercolour, 76.2 x 48.6 cm
British Columbia Archives, PDP 935

SOUTH BAY (Queen Charlotte Islands) 1928 (above)
Watercolour, 55.9 x 73.7 cm
Central Guaranty Trust, Toronto

Canada's very essence."[10] Clive Bell in *Art* (one of the books Harris had recommended to her) praised primitive art for its singleness of purpose and its absence of descriptive intent, and that message was also included in her article.

There were other signs of a growing interest in native art, even if the interest was strongly coloured by an awareness of its possibilities for attracting tourists. Such motivation was largely responsible for a program begun in the mid-1920s to restore poles in the Skeena valley on the Canadian National Railway route. Carr, in a letter to Eric Brown in 1928, deplored the method of restoration which, in covering the poles (moved from their original location to be more visible from the train station) with a uniform coat of grey paint, had robbed them of "interest and subtlety." Edwin Holgate's Totem Pole Room, designed for the CN's hotel Chateau Laurier in Ottawa in 1929, also attests to the growing appeal of the "noble savage."

If the Canadian context for seeing and thinking about this indigenous native heritage had shifted since Carr stopped working from native source material in 1913, her world view and her attitude to art had shifted even more as a result of her participation in that exhibition and her meeting with artists in eastern Canada in 1927. Her original intention to create a cumulative historical document had kept her art going for a long time, but it became increasingly divided after her exposure to French painting opened more painterly horizons for her. Now it was replaced by a new purpose: to produce works of expressive power.

Starting out at the end of June 1928, Carr made a second major trip north, intended to be even more ambitious and rewarding than that in 1912. (See Map B, page 229.) After stopping to visit Alert Bay, Fort Rupert and other Kwakiutl villages on Vancouver Island, she proceeded to the Skeena River area where she found that the poles had deteriorated greatly since her last visit and that those restored at Kitwanga had lost much of their character in the process. Kitwancool, an important site with fine poles, which she had not reached in 1912, was still several difficult miles off the new Canadian National Railway line now linking Edmonton with Prince Rupert, but she managed to get there and work from the exciting new material. For the first time, too, she reached the Nishga villages of Angida and Gitiks on the

AN INDIAN HOUSE, KOSKIMO VILLAGE 1930
Watercolour, 45.7 x 33 cm
Private collection

Nass River, an area recommended to her by Barbeau. Her visit to the Queen Charlotte Islands in 1912 had been richly rewarding and she looked forward to doing extensive work there a second time, but persistent bad weather curtailed her plans severely. Nonetheless, the sketching she was able to do at Skidegate, at South Bay across the inlet from Skidegate, on Maude Island and at the deserted village of Skedans was sufficient to provide her with material for several major canvases including OLD TIME COAST VILLAGE (South Bay) and VANQUISHED (Skedans). A letter she wrote Eric Brown, the National Gallery's director, on 11 August, a few days before her return to Victoria, is vivid with the experience of the trip, the hardships of travel and accommodation endured, including a near-fatal boat trip off Skedans during a storm, and attests to the commitment she was still prepared to make to the Indian material and the strength of the inner drive it reflected.

This was her last major trip to native settlements, though there were several shorter and, as it turned out, important expeditions: in early spring of 1929 she went to Nootka, a cannery community on an island off the west coast of Vancouver Island, and to nearby Friendly Cove where among the watercolours and drawings she did were those on which the famous canvas INDIAN CHURCH is based. In August of that year she went to Port Renfrew which resulted in a harvest of fine drawings. In mid-August of 1930, after stopping at Alert Bay, she made her way around the tip of Vancouver Island to the villages of Quatsino Sound, a last Indian trip which resulted in the well-known cat village painting and the related watercolour and drawing in the Vancouver Art Gallery collection, and in the story "D'Sonoqua" in *Klee Wyck*.

We get some idea of the prodigious amount of work done in many native village sites, and on all these trips between 1907 and 1930, from the drawings and watercolours in the Newcombe Collection in Victoria where well over three hundred of them (not all Indian) are held. There are small notebook drawings in pencil catching the compositional essence of a "scene" with its tilting poles in their village setting, viewed from one perspective and then from another, some of them bearing her notations for colour. There are watercolour notes of poles and details of pole sections or pole terminals, often several on the same sheet. There

KITWANCOOL 1928
Graphite drawing, 14.9 x 22.4 cm
British Columbia Archives, PDP 5779

will be multiple studies of the same pole, one catching its general character, another viewing it from a different position, others meticulously drawing or painting in the details of the pole's particular iconography. Through them we see her, no casual tourist-artist in search of superficial one-shot effects but the thorough-going student making repeated studies of her material as weather and accessibility permit, stocking her reservoir of information and experience. Sometimes the work reflects the speed with which adverse viewing conditions compelled her to do them, but always they respect the character of the carved and natural forms she was dealing with. Out of such layered and extended study a canvas might emerge representing the accumulated experience of several trips to the same location. In addition to the sketches done on the spot or studio work developed from them, there are dozens of drawings made from museum objects—canoes, woven hats, rattles, masks—some of them no doubt to be used as designs in the decoration of her pottery in the twenties but all of them serving to further engrave on her memory the characteristic forms of native art and something of their perceived underlying meaning. There are several drawings showing that she sometimes worked from photographs to supplement her information, a practice seen as a normal part of today's research process and in retrospect simply an indication of her quest for veracity when access to the original subjects was impossible. However, it should be mentioned that several of her Indian canvases were developed more directly from photographs. In her public talk of 1913 she vigorously denied using photographic aids in her work, an understandable statement at a time when such use by painters would have been regarded as a form of cheating in general and, for her in particular, a questioning of her claim to have studied her material firsthand. HOUSE FRONT, GOLD HARBOUR of 1913, HAINA and TOTEM VILLAGE of 1928 and BLUNDEN HARBOUR, 1930–32 have all been identified as originating in photographic sources, and there may be others. As a whole the Newcombe Collection stands as a testament to the seriousness and durability of her commitment and to the complexity and thoroughness of her working method.

By 1930 the actual native contacts were over. In any case, during the more than twenty years since she had first begun her

GUYASDOMS' D'SONOQUA C.1930
Oil on canvas, 100.3 x 65.4 cm
Art Gallery of Ontario, Toronto
Gift of Albert H. Robson Memorial Subscription Fund

quest, the moral and material deterioration of the native culture had reached a point that, even had her advancing age permitted them, further trips could have added little to her accumulated notes and sketches. These, with their overlay of her memories, were all she required to see her through her remaining need for Indian material.

Those memories were an important part of Carr's huge emotional investment in the Indian commitment and would soon come into play in her painting. Sketching the poles in their usually isolated and frequently difficult locations, always alone within the moment of artistic confrontation with her strange and exotic subjects, highly susceptible to the moods of weather and place, Carr's subjective experiences of these situations were vivid. She writes about her discovery of a carving of D'Sonoqua, the legendary "wild woman of the woods" of Kwakiutl myth, after pushing her way through a tangle of nettles, slipping off a slimy plank and finding the huge sculpture towering above her.

> She seemed to be part of the tree itself, as if she had grown there at its heart, and the carver had only chipped away the outer wood so that you could see her. . . . Now I saw her face. The eyes were two rounds of black, set in wider rounds of white, and placed in deep sockets under wide, black eyebrows. Their fixed stare bored into me as if the very life of the old cedar looked out, and it seemed that the voice of the tree itself might have burst from that great round cavity, with projecting lips, that was her mouth. Her ears were round, and stuck out to catch all sounds. The salt air had not dimmed the heavy red of her trunk and arms and thighs. Her hands were black, with blunt finger-tips painted a dazzling white. I stood looking at her for a long, long time. . . . The rain stopped, and white mist came up from the sea, gradually paling her back into the forest. It was as if she belonged there, and the mist were carrying her home. Presently the mist took the forest too, and, wrapping them both together, hid them away.[11]

In passages like the above, the drama and emotion of personal narrative is layered with a response to the carvings as strongly expressive presences on their own, a view of them as art opened up for her by her contact with Harris and the other easterners. They had substantiated her interest in native art and had enabled her to identify virtues in it that related to her vision of art. In the article she wrote for the June 1929 *McGill News Supplement,* she discusses native art, locating the native artist's creative intentions within her own. Giving Indian art what was for her its proper moral alignment, she points out that it is the "most 'modern' in spirit of anything in Canada." And the artists "have searched beneath the surface for the hidden thing which is felt rather than seen, the reality. . . which underlies everything."[12] She returns to this theme in a 1935 speech to Victoria Normal School students: "Their sensitiveness to design was magnificent; the originality and power of their art forceful, grand, . . . being taken from the very core of life itself."[13] Her attempt to put the native artist's intention into words sometimes gets off the mark, such as her claim for his "deep desire for self expression"; she forgot that the basic configurations of native art were set by tradition and adhered to by the individual artist whose personal feelings were not relevant. Such a slip is of no importance, for she is informing us of her own amplified intention, and that becomes clear in the great Indian paintings of this period.

No longer only an observer or a painterly eye, in the 1928–31 canvases Carr views the carvings from the romantic-dramatic perspective of her own highly charged experiences of them, seeing them as the stirring creations of a people of an imagined noble past, not in the abstraction of a museum hall but in their own evocative environment. And she is using pictorial lessons she had learned in France as well as all the relevant devices picked up from Harris, Tobey and her reading to heighten their express-iveness. The passages quoted above and the whole intention and painting attitude of these canvases—and indeed from 1928 on to the end—find their rationale in a paragraph, well-marked in Carr's copy, from Ralph Pearson's book. Supposing a particular instance in which the artist has posed a model to express sorrow, Pearson writes:

> The creative artist. . . begins to draw with his conceptual vision turned inwards searching the storehouse of his mind. That storehouse is well-stocked for he has made preliminary studies in plenty—probably has drawn a model accurately in order to pos-sess himself of all knowledge of details. And now he is ready to use his material to create a picture. The inner fire burns. He comes to his canvas filled with a suppressed power that urges hand to vital, swinging expression. Does he feel the bending weight of

sorrow? His hand flows the bend of sorrow into line. No thought of detail. Hardly a glance at the model. The *feel* of sorrow flowing into form! His problem becomes one of controlling the exuberance of spirit, of holding it to the slow, laborious process of organization, of conserving the force in him to hour after hour, and day after day, and week after week perhaps, of controlled release. . . . What was in him has gone into the work, where, 'if his power has been great enough', it will live forever. Thus is the felt nature of a thing eternalized into design.[14]

Those words, probably first read by Carr at the time of contact with Mark Tobey in 1928, describe precisely her own attitude to art as expressed in her talks and writing of this period and also in the new paintings that start to appear in 1928.

The Mature Indian Work

Watercolours done on that 1928 trip or developed from it, and which became the basis of canvases painted in the next three or four years, call on artistry so little used in the past fifteen years and reflect an already shifted attitude. In addition, some show the spirit of formal experimentation characterizing this time of search for means to meet new expressive demands. In QUEEN CHAR-LOTTE ISLANDS TOTEM the great beaver is powerfully present and confrontational, taking up most of the picture space, iconi-cally centred and monumental, pressed up close to the surface with no distancing foreground; in KISPIOX wolf and bear aggres-sively thrust their great overlapping heads into the picture space. INDIAN CHURCH, FRIENDLY COVE, one of three known water-colours relating to the famous canvas, and an untitled water-colour of an Angida pole have a strong basis of underlying drawing that emphasizes their aspect as formal exploration. In the latter, surrounding—almost engulfing—growth jerks and jags in a formal matrix that echoes the tension of the pole's creatures though successful melding of the two components is not quite achieved. Her old problem of finding a formal and representa-tional mode capable of including the poles in a unifying pictorial form has become more complex now that she requires the poles to take on a new expressiveness while retaining their integrity as objects. In another watercolour, KITWANCOOL, she found a bril-liant solution. A faceting vision—faintly reminiscent of Cézanne

THE INDIAN CHURCH, FRIENDLY COVE 1929
Watercolour and charcoal, 59.1 x 45.1 cm
Private collection

KITWANCOOL 1928
Watercolour, 75.4 x 56.3 cm
Vancouver Art Gallery, 42.3.100

Untitled (Angida) 1928
Watercolour, 75.3 x 27.8 cm
Vancouver Art Gallery, 42.3.99

QUEEN CHARLOTTE ISLANDS TOTEM
(Haina) d.1928 (below)
Watercolour, 75.8 x 53.3 cm
Vancouver Art Gallery, 42.3.97

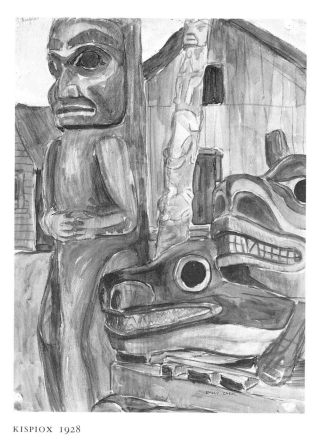

KISPIOX 1928
Watercolour, 75.4 x 56.5 cm
Vancouver Art Gallery, 42.3.105

THE CRYING TOTEM (Tanoo) 1928 (right)
Oil on canvas, 75.3 x 38.8 cm
Vancouver Art Gallery, 42.3.53

BRITISH COLUMBIA INDIAN VILLAGE
(Fort Rupert) 1930
Oil on canvas, 111.9 x 70.1 cm
Vancouver Art Gallery, 42.3.24

but realized in tone rather than colour—unifies poles, the ever-problematic sky, buildings and natural terrain in a common pictorial structure. In these watercolours Carr is already well advanced into the style and dramatic content of the major conceptual canvases that begin to appear shortly after the 1928 trip.

THE CRYING TOTEM is among several transitional canvases done early in 1928 (along with the previously discussed SKIDEGATE), when she had already broken away from her Post-Impressionist manner, but before her style assumed its authority under Tobey's influence. Following his visit she began to paint the well-known brooding canvases of these few years in which large Indian forms are placed in natural environments which provide stage sets for them or at times threaten to overwhelm them. In them she continues to find answers to the question of how to translate the confusion of the external visual world into pictorial terms now that she is working from a conceptual rather than a perceptual basis. The Indian carvings presented themselves to Carr as ready-made works of art, their process of creative formulation having long since been accomplished during centuries of cultural continuity. But what was to be the transformative mode of simplification for handling the proliferation of West Coast nature?

The outside sources of the stylistic ideas Carr used during this period have been discussed elsewhere, such as her formalization of sky or growth into solid echoes of cubo-futurist practice. Here we are more interested in the purposes to which Carr adapted those ideas which had to do with psychological expressiveness rather than formal investigation for its own sake.

There were essentially two kinds of native settings for which Carr had to find painting solutions: those where she could logically employ the dense forest backdrops of coastal settlement and those, as in the Skeena valley in more open settings, that called for an expanse of sky and less luxuriant growth. In either case, the mood needed to be strong and dramatic, in keeping with her rededication to the Indian's art based on a perception of its expressive character. In several canvases with expanses of open sky she employed a dynamic form construction, as in BIG RAVEN of 1931, where pendant clouds and light shafts are given volume and density, deep modelling and tonal contrast. BIG RAVEN and BRITISH COLUMBIA INDIAN VILLAGE (painted a few months

NIRVANA (Tanoo) 1929–30
Oil on canvas, 108.6 x 69.3 cm
Private collection

TANOO 1912 (right)
Watercolour, 74.9 x 52.7 cm
McMichael Canadian Art Collection,
Kleinburg, Ont.
Gift of Dr. and Mrs. Max Stern

earlier) are probably included in her thoughts when she wrote in her Journals, 19 March 1931: "I want to paint some skies so that they look roomy and moving and mysterious and to make them overhang the earth, to have a different quality in their distant horizon and their overhanging nearness."[15] Although painted in 1930, VANQUISHED too fits the description, the angles of its leaning poles and simplified curves of verdant terrain echoed in the sky's weighted diagonals and hanging dark clouds.

In canvases where rain forest provides the setting, dynamically composed sky is replaced by a microstructure of foliage formed, as it were, from thick slabs of dense green substance which may be carved and layered in small units—INDIAN CHURCH—or moulded into tongues of solid green flame—GUYASDOMS' D'SONOQUA.

Cubo-futurism's potential for transparency, which other artists had explored, would have had limited usefulness for Carr since the sombre and dramatic tone of her subjective experience of the Indian forms called for density, weight, enclosure and opacity. Now the assured masterminder, Carr shapes her paintings and the settings for poles for their expressive equivalence not their factual fidelity, as the comparison of a number of canvases with their earlier drawing or watercolour versions shows. The canvas NIRVANA (1929–30) is Carr's expression of the Buddhist state in which desires and passions are extinguished and the soul is absorbed into the supreme spirit—a reflection of the Buddhist component in theosophic doctrine which Carr was investigating at the time of painting. A comparison of the canvas with the studio watercolour TANOO of some eighteen years earlier shows how she has intensified the drama: the sky is crowded out, detail disappears (moss on the Raven's head, particulars of foliage) and so do the touches of bright colour, and in the cloistered and dimly lit world of the canvas the poles take on their new meaning.

The "stands" of poles in open space that Carr painted in her Post-Impressionist period disappear after 1928 (unless one includes VANQUISHED among them), giving way to free-standing figural carvings such as welcome figures, D'Sonoquas or memorial posts brought close up into the picture space; and being less iconographically complicated than a crest pole with its assembled crowd of diverse creatures, they usually had clear

BIG RAVEN (Cumshewa) 1931
Oil on canvas, 87.3 x 114.4 cm
Vancouver Art Gallery, 42.3.11

expressive possibilities for her to realize, as in POTLATCH WEL-
COME or GUYASDOMS' D'SONOQUA. BIG RAVEN is based on material from her 1912 trip to Cumshewa where a monumental
carving of a raven still marked the location of a mortuary house
for Haidas who had died in the great smallpox epidemic of the
1860s. In *Klee Wyck* Carr recalled the 1912 experience in which
she had first sketched "the dilapidated old raven" left alone
without his mate to watch over dead Indian bones; the memory
of it was one of "great lonesomeness smothered in a blur of
rain."[16] The canvas presents not only the pole but the entire
experience—the looming monumental presence of the bird, her
perception of its lonely and grand vigil, the appropriately
threatening sky, and the encircling swirl of growth at its base.
The 1912 studio watercolour of the same subject, CUMSHEWA,
bears a close compositional resemblance and already has a mood
of considerable drama. But we note that the oil has exchanged the
decorative elegance of art nouveau curves in the watercolour's
foreground vegetation for a threatening tidal wave of green, and
has in fact tuned all the elements to their maximum theatrical
intensity without crossing the line into melodrama.

Always giving the new vision its full pictorial and emotional
effectiveness in the density of the oil medium, some of the Indian
canvases of these few years develop out of the crop of late watercolours and drawings while others show her carrying the same
theme forward over a period of time and enriching it with her
own fresh experience as her work evolved. VANQUISHED is one
of the major canvases that represents the culmination of an
extended involvement with a particular Indian site, Skedans. In
1912 she first visited the abandoned village with its one remaining
standing house and wealth of poles, stretched around the
southern bay of a narrow-necked peninsula which ends in the
characteristic rocky prominence seen in her paintings. Conditions
had been good on that first trip, as she tells her story in *Klee
Wyck*, and she made many drawings and watercolours from
which she subsequently developed studio watercolours and at
least two fine canvases, one of which was in the 1927 Ottawa
exhibition. "The bitter-sweet of [the] overwhelming loneliness"
she experienced in the Queen Charlotte Islands villages urged her
back a second time in 1928 when, at Skedans, she found the wild

POTLATCH WELCOME (Mimquimlees) 1930
Oil on canvas, 110.5 x 67.2 cm
Art Gallery of Ontario, Toronto
Bequest of Charles S. Band

CUMSHEWA 1912
Watercolour, 52 x 75.5 cm
National Gallery of Canada

VANQUISHED (Skedans) 1930
Oil on canvas, 92.0 x 129 cm
Vancouver Art Gallery, 42.3.6

INDIAN HUT, QUEEN CHARLOTTE ISLANDS
(Cumshewa) 1930
Oil on canvas, 101.6 x 81.9 cm
National Gallery of Canada
The Vincent Massey bequest

COMMUNAL HOUSE (Mimquimlees) 1908–09
Watercolour, 25.4 x 33.7 cm
British Columbia Archives, PDP 920

SKEDANS 1928 (top)
Graphite drawing, 15.1 x 50.4 cm
British Columbia Archives, PDP 8936

Untitled (Welcome Figure, Mimquimlees) c. 1912
Watercolour, 34.3 x 25.4 cm
Private collection

THE CROOKED STAIRCASE (Mimquimlees) 1928–30
Oil on canvas, 109.2 x 66.7 cm
The Vancouver Club, Vancouver
Gift of H. R. MacMillan

growth rapidly obliterating every trace of man: "Now only a few hand-hewn cedar planks and roof beams remained, moss-grown and sagging—a few totem poles, greyed and split."[17] Despite rain, storm and anxiety for the safety of the native's boat that had brought her, she managed in a few hours to make some sketchbook drawings on which a watercolour and this large canvas—which powerfully sublimes her accumulated experience of Skedans—were based. Another such canvas is THE CROOKED STAIRCASE. The subject, from the village of Mimquimlees on Village Island, a theatrical welcome figure and a house whose gabled roof is topped with a large carved raven, first drew her attention in 1908 or 1909, as recorded in a small watercolour in the British Columbia Archives, Victoria, from which she subsequently developed a colourful Post-Impressionist canvas in 1912. To those two works can be added a watercolour drawing of the figure (which she gave to Mark Tobey in the 1920s) as well as a related quick drawing-book sketch, all part of the imaginative holding and enfolding process which culminated in the last dramatic canvas.

In the best of these Indian canvases—INDIAN CHURCH, BIG RAVEN, NIRVANA, GUYASDOM'S D'SONOQUA among others—all past hesitancies have been overcome, all combined influences have been fused in a powerful vision of her own: that of the Group of Seven, in the bigness and boldness of conception; of Lawren Harris, in the simplified mode and the emphasis on design; of Tobey, in guiding her to a structural approach capable of meshing with her emerging vision, and in those books that provided models and instruction in simplification enabling her to move into a symbolic mode of painting.

Why did Carr leave the Indian theme after 1931? Harris's suggestion that she do so offers a simple answer. In a letter undated but probably from the late fall of 1929, he suggested that she leave the poles alone for a year or more because the "totem is a work of art in its own right and it is very difficult to use it in another form of art. But," he wrote, "how about seeking an equivalent for it in the exotic landscape of the Island and coast, making your own form and forms with the greater form."[18] Tobey also gave her similar advice to leave the Indians and poles and to paint from inside herself, and doubtless such counsel had its effect.

OLD TIME COAST VILLAGE (South Bay) 1929–30
Oil on canvas, 91.3 x 128.7 cm
Vancouver Art Gallery, 42.3.4

But such paintings as TOTEM AND FOREST, INDIAN CHURCH and OLD TIME COAST VILLAGE, paintings showing a thematic balance between nature and Indian, and which were done at the same time as a handsome series of canvases in which the forest itself is explored, raise the possibility of less literal reasons. Carr, who admits that in the early days she sketched the Indian material "in a desultory way just for the joy of it,"[19] now understood through her own experience what that material was about—not from anthropologists' explanations but from the understanding that years of studying their form and responding to them in their environment had given her. She felt the overall expressive character of native art: its tightness, its restraint, its inner tension, its mysterious, sober and dark spirit that was sometimes daemonic, sometimes quiescent. And so she took on the Indian's darkness in her canvases, closing them in with weighty and darkened skies, or with claustrophobic forests even when fidelity to her subject did not require her to do so. In seeking out the poles in their abandoned and overgrown locations and in creating painted environments that empathized with their character, she was drawn deeply into nature's dark side. And in probing one aspect of nature so deeply there opened up for her a vision of nature that embraced all moods, a possibility not previously envisioned. It is at a certain point that her paintings themselves tell us how, after her prolonged familiarity with Indian art and through her own painting-act in creating equivalent nature environments, she intuitively grasped the sense in which Indian art was an expression of the native's relation to the natural and supernatural world as he understood it, and to his environment of which it was a particular part. Metaphorically speaking, in forming a nature responsive to the native's art she made the bigger discovery: that he had before her distilled his art from "nature." To recognize the symbolizing process of art as she had instinctively come to do was a liberation, for it was the most profound secret that Indian art (or any other) could yield. At that point she was finished with native art so to speak; having penetrated its secret in understanding she had no further need of it. And it had confirmed for her the direction in which she was already heading: towards nature.

Such insights on Carr's part, whether she articulated them or

STRANGLED BY GROWTH (Koskimo) 1931
Oil on canvas, 64 x 48.6 cm
Vancouver Art Gallery, 42.3.42

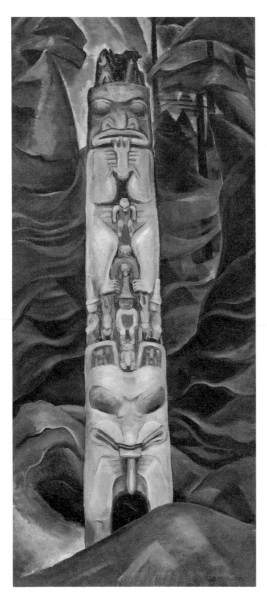

TOTEM AND FOREST
(Tow Hill pole, Q.C.I.) 1931
Oil on canvas, 129.3 x 56.2 cm
Vancouver Art Gallery, 42.3.1

not, are implicit in several works of this period. No attempt should be made to deduce a sequential evolution from them; the period under discussion is short and concentrated and for Carr, as for most artists, the surfacing or temporary disappearance of important ideas follows the imagination's own order. Carr may not have seen the pole of TOTEM AND FOREST in the forest setting she gave it, a canvas which speaks of a symbolic rather than literal relation between its components. She likens the forest to the pole in composition (two narrow vertical sections of forest similar in shape and size to the pole), in tone and colour affinity and in imagery, for the forest—with its weaving undersea of forms that mouth and peer—seems but a poetic transposition of the mysterious life of the pole to that of the forest. In such an interchange of imaging between pole and forest, the act of transformation, which in the realm of native mythology permits creatures to don another identity by slipping from one skin into another, finds an equivalence. In the small canvas STRANGLED BY GROWTH the wild spirit of man as exemplified in the mythical D'Sonoqua, which belongs to the dark forces of the Indian's universe, glares menacingly through lashings of untamed forest tangle, a restatement of the inherent, contained tension of Northwest Coast Indian art. Again in this dramatic canvas, Indian and nature are one in spirit.

Carr's long ago communication with that old Indian chieftain by means of an exchange of staring finds a particular resonance in a few of her late Indian works. The eyes in Indian art are "always exaggerated because the supernatural beings could see everywhere, and see more than we could," Carr observed in her 1935 public lecture.[20] The sightless, staring eyes that are so prominent a feature in native art project a sense of silent inner watching which finds its metaphoric equivalence in the dark depths of silent forests. Or it could be put the other way around equally well, and this was the striking discovery that Carr made and now projected in her work. In an untitled charcoal drawing of 1929 parts of a pole or poles—the heads of an eagle and a beaver—poke out from dense and highly abstracted tree forms. In a closely related second drawing the carving has lost its integrity as object, and its details—the Raven's head and beak, the generic "ovoid" form motif of native design, the eye—are absorbed into a mutual exis-

Untitled (totemic faces in stylized forest) 1929–30
Charcoal drawing, 62.7 x 47.8 cm
Vancouver Art Gallery, 42.3.129

Untitled (formalized tree forms
with totemic details) 1929–30
Charcoal drawing, 62.6 x 47.9 cm
Vancouver Art Gallery, 41.2.123

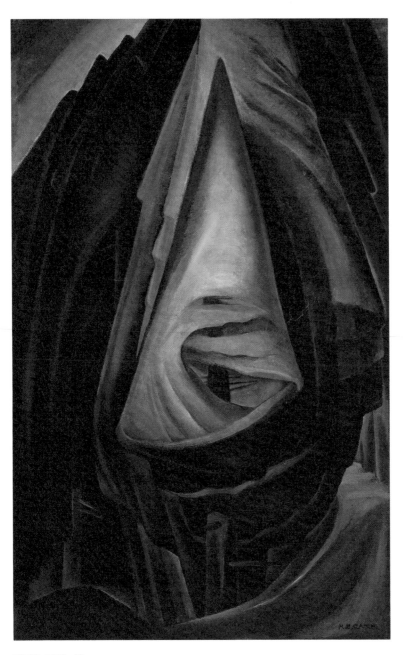

GREY 1929–30
Oil on canvas, 106.7 x 68.9 cm
Private collection

tence with the forest. The supernatural Indian eye has become the mythic "eye" of the forest. We might say that Carr has gone through the eye of the Indian and come out into the forest, into nature.

A witness to the completion of this internal rite of passage is the painting GREY in which the locale of "watching presence" is shifted to the forest itself. In GREY there is no Indian form, though much of the Indian spirit is there: a dim and enfolded world, an iconic confronting silence, a symbolic eye, a glimpse into the secret inner heart of the timeless placeless forest. In no work do we find a stronger or more poetic statement of Carr's mystical participation in the dark and haunted spirit of the forest to which the Indian had awakened her. She was now free to move her art into other areas of nature's expression with a deepened sense of identification.

There was a postscript to the long affair with the Indian. In 1937, at the age of sixty-six, Carr had a serious heart attack which involved a stay in hospital and a lengthy convalescence. Her painting activity, temporarily interrupted, prompted her to turn to her writing, which had been an alternative occupation for some years. Going back over her Indian stories recalled all the Indian experiences, and when she was able to return to painting, she began a group of Indian canvases. Barely out of hospital she reported, "I have been painting all day, with four canvases on the go—Nass pole in undergrowth, Koskimo, Massett bear, and an exultant wood."[21] Again in May 1941 she wrote to a friend: "Going over Indian sketches [stories] has stirred up a homesick-ness for Indian."[22] The Nass pole referred to is certainly the well-known FORSAKEN in the Vancouver Art Gallery's collection (which also includes a late Masset canvas). In 1941 preparation for the publication of her Indian stories, which make up *Klee Wyck*, her first book, included the idea of a coincident exhibition of her painting. The exhibition did not materialize, but LAUGHING BEAR, one of several paintings stimulated by her interest in the book, was painted for her publisher and appeared on the cover of the first paperback edition. It, like the other late Indian paintings, was worked up from material gathered earlier, in this case a 1928 visit to Gitiks where she could see only the bear's back because

LAUGHING BEAR (Angida) 1941
Oil on paper, 76.6 x 55.3 cm
Private collection

of the tangle of growth but nonetheless captured his "merry" expression.[23]

A late painting, one of two of 1941–42, where she again achieves a fusion between nature and the Indian form, not in the dark and heavy mood of earlier times but in the spirit of flowing energy that animates her subsequent work, forms a fitting conclusion to her long love affair with the Indian and will be discussed in the following section.

TREES IN THE SKY C.1939
Oil on canvas, 111.76 x 68.48 cm
Private collection

6 From Landscape to Nature's Transcendence

Dictionary definitions of the word "landscape" vary, but they all depend on two conditions: a viewer standing or sitting (some-place here) and a viewed configuration of nature (someplace out there). Viewing is always implied, that is, the conscious attitude of observation on the part of the subject rather than a general reference to the kinds of seeing that may occur when the eyes are inattentively open; and also implied is the passive self-display on the part of the observed hills, clouds, stands of trees or whatever. A certain distance or detachment between the viewer and the viewed, both spatial and attitudinal, is suggested. The word's meaning in art of course may be and has been expanded to the bursting point to cover altered concepts of nature and any number of imaginable variations on the relation between the observer (artist) and the perceived. But for the purposes of discussing Carr's work, the narrower conventional understanding of landscape will be kept in mind to distinguish her earlier attitude towards nature from her late work where the detachment between observer and observed transforms into a relationship of intimacy and, finally, identification.

Early Landscape; Assertion of Nature

Even if Carr had not had an inborn attachment to nature, it was to be expected that many of her early paintings should be

Untitled (forest pool with cattle) d.1909
Watercolour, 54 x 36.8 cm
Private collection

GIANT TREES, STANLEY PARK (Vancouver) d.1909 (right)
Watercolour on paper laid down on masonite,
63.5 x 47.6 cm
Private collection

landscapes since that was an assumed mode for artists at the time. In choosing her subjects, more often than not she acceded to the Victorians' taste for the parklike areas in which the city abounded—scenes that spoke of leisurely outdoor activity with easy space for the spectator to step into and without reminders of nature's harsher realities: open meadows prettied by flowers, winding streams, vistas across the water. If mountains were required, they were suitably distanced or reduced in scale in a concept tamed to the preferences of their expected audience.

Even so, among Carr's early paintings are some of undomesticated scenery—large trees, forest paths—which hint at an innate feeling for nature as something more than an appealing outdoor view, as a force projecting its own range of moods and expressions. A watercolour of 1909 is characteristically domesticated for us by two foreground cows browsing by a pool while a rail fence threads through the stand of trees in the background. But she has injected a touch of grandeur into this fairly small painting of an ordinary scene through her handling of the interior scale, the tiny painted forms of animals in contrast with the large and lumbering creatures of our mental images of them and the trees given their full dimension of height and massiveness. A stronger hint of the Carrs to come is to be found in several paintings of the same time—1909 or 1910—done in Vancouver while she was teaching there before her stay in France. There are at least three watercolours and an oil painted in Vancouver's famous Stanley Park that deal with the theme of the dim "cathedral like" forest interior lit by shafts of light filtering down through foliage far overhead. This theme, frequently used in her later painting, lends itself to sentimental treatment, and bad painters the world over have effectively trivialized it for many viewers; but we would be mistaken to pass by such a work as GIANT TREES, STANLEY PARK. Although it is painted with a straightforward naturalism that interests us less than her more inventive later approaches, it represents the same keen observation and direct response to a particular statement of nature that characterizes the best of her nature paintings. Here it happens to carry a mood and is free of the deliberate evocation of sentiment through the addition of a gratuituous comment of her own of which she was occasionally guilty. The totality of her response to the place is also communicated in

BRITTANY LANDSCAPE 1911
Oil on cardboard, 44.1 x 61.3 cm
Private collection

AUTUMN IN FRANCE 1911 (top)
Oil on cardboard, 49 x 65.9 cm
National Gallery of Canada

BRITTANY, FRANCE 1911
Oil on canvas, 46.8 x 61.8 cm
McMichael Canadian Art Collection,
Kleinburg, Ont.

ALONG THE CLIFF, BEACON HILL (Victoria) d.1919
Oil on cardboard, 37.6 x 45.3 cm
Private collection

her words as she recalls the experience in *Growing Pains*: "Alone, I went there to sketch, loving its solitudes—no living creature but dog Billie and me, submerged beneath a drown of undergrowth. Above us were gigantic spreads of pines and cedar boughs, no bothersome public, no rubbernoses. Occasional narrow trails wound through bracken and tough salal tangle. Underfoot, rotting logs lay, upholstered deep in moss, bracken, forest wastage. Your feet never knew how deep they would sink."[1] The Stanley Park paintings also point ahead to the communication of aloneness in and intimacy with nature which characterizes much of her later work.

The paintings of the Brittany countryside done in France represent simply a part of the wealth of new subject material offered to her quickened eyes, along with scenes of human activity in cottage interiors or farmyards, country churches or whatever, for she was there to learn a new way of painting and to clear her eyes of their old world vision, not to clarify or deepen her content. So landscapes like AUTUMN IN FRANCE or the BRITTANY LANDSCAPE of the 1911 Salon d'Automne showing in Paris, tell us of her exuberance and adeptness in the new mode, yet the relation to nature is still that of the landscape painter. These are fine and highly accomplished paintings, but in the context of the present discussion what interests us particularly is the immediacy and freedom of brush and the rhythmic swing of their compositions. In AUTUMN IN FRANCE, brilliant with its touches of red under green, yellow, violet, blue and orange, short firm chopping strokes follow the directional contours of field, hill, cliff and sky activating the surface into a vibrancy of light and at the same time organizing the picture space into larger movements that roll in response to each other. Her later work will echo such directness and rhythm.

The paintings done in her fifteen years of discouragement and reduced production following her year in France are all landscapes, though landscapes moving into the realm of nature painting. We know twenty or so of them and there may not have been many more—a likely average of less than two paintings a year. They show no lapse of painterly authority though their consistent small scale reflects a diminished ambition, and whereas a few are dated there are not enough of them to form the basis for a

Untitled (trees against whirling sky) 1913–15
Oil on canvas, 57.2 x 48.3 cm
Private collection

clear pattern of change or development. They do, however, begin to show a marked departure from the style she had used to paint the ordered countryside of France now that she was back in the moisture-softened atmosphere of Victoria on Canada's West Coast and responding to the kind of landscape that attracted her. Frequently painted from Beacon Hill Park, they show the cliffs with a tumble of driftwood at their base, an open grove of trees or a single tree—in several paintings, the West Coast's orange-trunked arbutus in a close-up study or clinging to the cliff edge and seen against the sea and sky. The character of the brushwork and colour of a small, dazzling, untitled sketch of arbutus trees against a brilliant sky—broken, vibrant and high-keyed—suggests a date early in the decade while the impact of the French experience was still strongly with her. Its swirling, ecstatic sky, tossing trees and erupted hillside embody the spirit of animation in nature that relates it to works she will do some twenty years later. Three related paintings of cliff and foreshore, one of which, ALONG THE CLIFF, BEACON HILL, is dated 1919, continue the painterly approach but with a disappearance of the broken directional brush stroke in favour of larger rolling masses of rich but somewhat muted colour. In ARBUTUS TREE, dated 1922, and several other studies of single trees—the sturdy-trunked Garry oak or one of the West Coast conifers—the ornate negative spaces carved out by strongly contoured trunks, branches and clumps of foliage are filled in with positive chunks and wedges of colour, flattening the picture into a rich tapestry of pigment. In an untitled painting of a tree on a rocky profile, Carr's exuberant seizure of the ruggedness of her subject—its simplified and bold forms, the directness of the painting, the steep angle of the cliff's profile, and the massiveness of the boulders of which it is composed—suggests a striking affinity with work of the Group of Seven a decade earlier though she was not to see it until the end of the twenties. In all these paintings we see Carr moving somewhat uncertainly from one variant of the Post-Impressionist idiom to another though always painting with vigour, and always now reacting to the character of her subject rather than simply imposing a stylistic vision or a manner upon it.

During the four or so years of Carr's concentrated production following her moral and artistic regeneration through contact

ARBUTUS TREE d. 1922
Oil on canvas, 45.9 x 35.6 cm
Private collection
Intended gift to the National Gallery
Bequest of Thomas Gardiner Keir

Untitled (tree on rocky profile) 1922–27
Oil on canvas, 41 x 56.2 cm
Private collection

Untitled (South Bay, Q.C.I.) c.1929
Oil on canvas, 58.4 x 68.6 cm
Private collection

SEA DRIFT AT THE EDGE OF THE FOREST c.1931 (left)
Oil on canvas, 112.4 x 68.9 cm
Vancouver Art Gallery, 42.3.25

with the Group of Seven and Mark Tobey, the Indian element predominated in her paintings, though, as we have already seen, nature was playing a vital supportive role in the total concept. Even when for Carr the Indian forms dissolved into nature—absorbed, one might say, back into their environment as they were beginning to do around 1930—the mood and kind of nature they had helped reveal to her continued for a while to characterize her nature paintings. A comparison of the 1928 watercolour SOUTH BAY with the untitled oil painting she developed from it shows how she has totally transformed the experience of the watercolour into her dark and brooding mode, solidifying and formalizing the foliage, deciding against a psychological release to the sky and closing in the space: the expressive artist who was still "thinking Indian" adjusting the more detached perspective of the observing artist who had sketched the scene on the spot out-of-doors. She has also in this canvas tipped the Indian-nature balance in favour of nature, virtually eliminating the signs of native habitation, the few small buildings centre right having been melded into the larger tonality and colouration. Dark and densely foliaged forest interiors or confronting walls of opaque growth with their corresponding moods of claustrophobia and forbidding soberness continue to characterize such paintings as WESTERN FOREST, FOREST, BRITISH COLUMBIA and SEA DRIFT AT THE EDGE OF THE FOREST. Apart from outside influences from Tobey or anyone else, the inventiveness and the mastery of pictorial form directed towards a particular intent shown here develop out of her own tireless exploration of the forms of nature, and we can see the kind and extent of her study underlying such works in the large number of drawings she did in 1929 and 1930.

Drawing was a natural habit with Carr, and she worked from whatever subjects interested her at the time including in her earlier days her animals or herself, usually pictured in some amusing predicament. Throughout her life she produced innumerable drawings from nature in pencil, charcoal or brush, ranging from small sketchbook drawings or scrap paper notations, on which a detail of foliage or the swing of a tree or a particular form relationship is explored, to more developed compositions. The Newcombe Collection in Victoria covers the extent of such drawings

Untitled ("rhythm, weight, space, force") c.1930
Graphite on paper, 14.9 x 22.5 cm
British Columbia Archives, PDP 8794

Untitled (tree, drooping branches) 1929 (left)
Graphite drawing, 22.5 x 14.9 cm
British Columbia Archives, PDP 5709

Untitled (tree rhythms) c.1929 (top)
Graphite drawing, 22.5 x 14.9 cm
British Columbia Archives, PDP 5842

(as it does of the Indian subjects) while the Vancouver Art Gallery's collection has a number of those that were carefully developed and brought to completion. Together they constitute an important and relatively little-known body of her work.

Carr was carrying the two contents—Indian and nature—forward at the same time in her work, shifting from one focus to the other or balancing them evenly, when she made her last three excursions to native areas on the broken outer coast of northwestern Vancouver Island: Nootka and Friendly Cove (where the Indian Church was located) and Port Renfrew in 1929, Quatsino Sound in 1930. Although these trips provided her with some Indian material, they were far richer in experiences of nature. In a section of her unpublished journal she speaks ecstatically about, and writes a rhapsodic poem of, her time in the woods in Port Renfrew, and she writes again of her forest experience in Quatsino: "What do these forests make you feel? Their weight and density, their crowded order. . . there is scarcely room for another tree and yet there is space around each. They are profoundly solemn yet upliftingly joyous. . . the juice and essence of life are in them and they teem with life, growth and expansion, they are a haven of refuge for myriads of living things."[2]

The wealth of remarkable drawings from these late excursions came in the couple of years immediately following the inspirational charge and the practical lessons she received from Harris and Tobey respectively, inspiration and lessons which she had to work out in her painting on her own. The drawings are memorable in themselves and for what they tell us about the thoughtful, intelligent, tirelessly probing, inventive artist not always suspected behind the passionate spontaneity of her late work. First came sketchbook drawings, dozens of them, usually pencil, done on the manila pages of ordinary soft-covered, stitched drawing-books. The small format of the pages is perfectly suited to their concentrated and synoptic vision and to their character as unequivocal statements of artistic intention. They are intensely thoughtful drawings, the mind sorting and organizing the chaos of natural data delivered by the eye and directing the willing hand: trees are given distinctive shape, direction and mass, transformed into compositional motifs or welded into

Untitled (structured tree forms) c. 1929
Graphite drawing, 22. 5 x 14. 9 cm
British Columbia Archives, PDP 5853

Untitled (beach, sea) c. 1930 (top)
Graphite on paper, 14. 9 x 22. 5 cm
British Columbia Archives, PDP 5633

Untitled (stylized island in cartouche) c. 1929 (left)
Graphite drawing, 22. 5 x 14. 9 cm
British Columbia Archives, PDP 5739

larger compositions; the cascading tumble of thick foliage in a stand of trees is reformulated in a nearly abstract zigzag of a few pencil strokes; a single line, moving easily but unerringly from point to strategic point in a simple geometric configuration states a whole structural theme. In one striking drawing a couple of dozen fluid lines delineate a deep inlet enclosed by rolling hills and streaming sky—or more accurately and on a different level of representation, as her words written across the top indicate, they designate "rhythm, weight, space, force." Another presents a very designed island seen as though through a camera's "fish-eye" lens, the contours of its shoreline, receding rocks, hump of overlapping trees and answering bands of sky fitting within the drawn and enclosing cartouche which "islands" the image on the page. This drawing, like many of the others, confirms the discovery in her own experience of the concept of nature-as-sculpture, a concept that Harris, Tobey and Pearson had introduced to her.

These are Carr's investigations into the rich, visual architecture of the natural environment, its large and small patterns of structure and energy and movement, as assiduously carried out as those of researchers in any field and with her artist's imagination in full power. Her study of the Indian poles had been equally careful and multilayered but since they represented material that had already been given order and shape, the problems they presented were of a different kind.

These small sketchbook drawings of 1929 and 1930 are the basis for a group of studio drawings done at the same time but of larger format, on either full or half sheets of usually better quality paper. Carefully worked out as compositions that take into account the full area of the picture space, and marked by a high degree of finish and conceptual clarity, they are consumate works on their own which together constitute a unique group in Carr's larger oeuvre. Whether her excited discovery of nature's rich revelation of form possibilities simply impelled her into such fully developed statements or whether she needed to consolidate her ideas before taking them into her painting, they give us a revealing glimpse into her working method and her creative process.

She was still under the spell of the Indian presence and in

NOOTKA 1929
Charcoal drawing, 72.1 x 53.8 cm
Vancouver Art Gallery, 42.3.118

Untitled (landscape with "eye" in sky) 1930
Charcoal drawing, 48.3 x 63.2 cm
Vancouver Art Gallery, 42.3.136

PORT RENFREW 1929 (left)
Charcoal drawing, 64.6 x 50.8 cm
Vancouver Art Gallery, 42.3.120

WOOD INTERIOR 1929–30
Oil on canvas, 106.68 x 69.9 cm
Robert McLaughlin Gallery, Oshawa
Gift of Miss Isabel McLaughlin

several of these drawings she expressed the underlying correspondence that she had discovered between the natural environment and the Indian carvings in which eyes, or eyelike shapes,
appear between totemlike sections of foliage. As she would still
say in 1933, when she was sketching in Goldstream Flats under
those mighty primeval cedars, "you sense the Indian and brave,
fine spiritual things."[3] Was she aware of the "eye" she had drawn
in the sky of an untitled landscape (VAG 42.3.136), or of the
"mask" lying at the base of tree trunks in the forest interior in
PORT RENFREW, a drawing which relates to the lyrical canvas
WOOD INTERIOR?

The drawings of these two years—the small direct sketches and
the large charcoals—represent Carr's liberal "stocking the
storehouse of her mind" of Pearson's advice. In them she developed the prototypes for many of the ideas and nature themes that
would appear in her work from now on: the tree as a stable
vertical around which whorls of branches circle upwards or from
which hang the drapelike curtain of foliage that we see in the
cedar tree drawings of 1931; the whirling spiral of a young
evergreen; the naked tree bole; the writhing stump; the living
wall of jungle, and the opening into the woods.

Movement and Space

STRANGLED BY GROWTH and BIG RAVEN (both February 1931)
mark the end of Carr's preoccupation with the Indian presence.
As the great carvings disappear they withdraw their dark and forbidding hold over nature too. This is the beginning of the last
great years in which she is free to express the whole range of
experience that she finds in nature and in herself—the dark side
still at times but also the exuberance, the freedom and openness,
the joy.

The range of nature from which she now chooses her subjects
extends beyond the deep forest (though that is still included) to
light second-growth woods, open fields, airy tree tops, sweeping
skies, driftwood beaches beneath worn cliffsides, logged-off
hillsides—an extension of territory dictated by the new governing paradigm which from now on will direct her work: everything must be alive, nothing static. The word she uses most often
to sum up the animating principle is "movement."

Untitled (cedar tree) 1931
Charcoal drawing, 92.7 x 61.4 cm
Vancouver Art Gallery, 42.3.114

SHORELINE d.1936
Oil on canvas, 68.6 x 111.5 cm
McMichael Canadian Art Collection,
Kleinburg, Ont.
Gift of Mrs. H. P. DePencier

CORDOVA DRIFT 1931 (top)
Oil on canvas, 74.9 x 90.2 cm
Private collection

A main movement must run through the picture. The transitions must be easy, not jerky. None must be out of step in the march. On, on, deeper and deeper, with the soul of the thing burrowing into its depths and intensity till that thing is a reality to us and speaks one grand inaudible word—God. The movement and direction of lines and planes shall express some attribute of God— power, peace, strength, serenity, joy. The movement shall be so great the picture will rock and sway together, carrying the artist and after him the looker with it, catching up with the soul of the thing and marching on together.[4]

Again in the same vein less than a year later:

I woke up this morning with "unity of movement" in a picture strong in my mind. I believe Van Gogh had that idea. . . . It seems to me that clears up a lot. I see it very strongly out on the beach and cliffs. I felt it in the woods but did not quite realize what I was feeling. Now it seems to me the first thing to seize on in your layout is the direction of your main movement, the sweep of the whole thing as a unit. One must be very careful about the transition of one curve of direction into the next, vary the length of the wave of space but *keep it going*, a pathway for the eye and the mind to travel through and into the thought. For long I have been trying to get the movement of the parts. Now I see there is only *one* movement. It sways and ripples. It may be slow or fast but it is only one movement sweeping out into space but always keeping going—rocks, sky, one continuous movement.[5]

The following year she writes:

A picture equals a movement in space. Pictures have swerved too much towards design and decoration. . . . The idea must run through the whole, the story that arrested you and urged the desire to express it, the story that God told you through that com- bination of growth. The picture side of the thing is the relation- ship of the objects to each other in one concerted movement, so that the whole gets up and goes, lifting the looker with it, sky sea, trees affecting each other. Lines at right angles hold the eye fixed. Great care should be taken in the articulation of one movement into another so that the eye swings through the whole canvas with a continuous movement and does not find jerky stops, though it may be bucked occasionally with quick little turns to accelerate the motion of certain places. One must ascertain first whether your subject is a slow lolling one, or smooth flowing and serene, or quick and jerky, or heavy and ponderous.[6]

These statements on the subject of movement are representative of the many Carr made in speaking of her essential intent for the art she produced after 1931–32; movement is to determine the pictorial character of the work ("the picture-side of the thing") and to represent the God-side of the thing, the meaning immanent in that particular segment of nature or "combination of growth." They also hint at the universality of her concept of nature, and at the knowing artist–craftsperson constantly aware of her painting strategies.

Movement indeed became a major component in Carr's work once she was fully immersed in nature, though it was already conspicuously present in the coils, spurts and cascades of growth and writhing roots in the Indian paintings of 1930 and 1931. Several canvases, done while she was in the sculptural mode the carvings had prompted but without their actual dominating presence, are characterized by the deep, heavy, continuous rhythms we find in FOREST, BRITISH COLUMBIA or DEEP FOREST or the South Bay canvas; or by the enfolding and falling layers of drapery of A YOUNG TREE. These paintings invoke something of the spirit of slumbrous, slow, erotic stirring and awakening, of things half-emerging, that one finds in Buddhist rock-carving, dimly visible in the deep tenebrous caves of Elora or Elephanta. Movement is now established as the governing principle and will be presented in various forms over the next seven or eight years. There is the "smooth flowing and serene" movement of THE RED CEDAR and of very late paintings like CEDAR SANCTUARY and there is her "heavy and ponderous" movement—the titanic power that bends the rim of the ocean, that tilts the plane of the sea, that arcs the sky to the earth's roundness, that twists the giant cedar roots and tosses them on heaving beaches, that pushes the wall of forest to sea edge. Such energy getting inside and under the forms of nature, like a giant swell at sea under a ship, is what we find in SHORELINE or CORDOVA DRIFT. There is as well the powerful movement that surges through stands of trees, through undergrowth, through skies—not a matter of masses themselves in motion but the rippling or quivering as a pervasive current courses through them. In such cases "energy" may be a better term than "movement" to cover both what happens on the painting surface and to the meaning within, that is, the painting's intended symbolic nature as signifying the animating force

THE RED CEDAR 1931–33
Oil on canvas, 111 x 68.5 cm
Vancouver Art Gallery, 54.7
Gift of Mrs. Ella Fell

A YOUNG TREE c.1931 (right)
Oil on canvas, 112 x 68.5 cm
Vancouver Art Gallery, 42.3.18

CEDAR SANCTUARY C.1942
Oil on paper, 91.5 x 61 cm
Vancouver Art Gallery, 42.3.71

DEEP FOREST C.1931
Oil on canvas, 69.3 x 111.8 cm
Vancouver Art Gallery, 42.3.16

immanent in all creation. Energy may also be better suited to refer to some of the kinds of vitality that now are determining the life of her paintings, energy that is not necessarily linear or directional. In some paintings we find skies that throb as with an electric charge, perhaps holding upright within their pulsing energy the forms of spindly trees left behind as rejects in the loggers' harvesting. In ABOVE THE TREES the sky vibrates in large circling traces which echo the whirling of the treetops. When faced with a great immobile cliff that "has the heavy cumbersomeness [of] the hindquarters of a bear,"[7] she animates its surface and whirls the sky that tucks down behind it. Movement, or energy, has become a transforming lens through which she perceives her world.

Space was the second term in Carr's new equation—"a painting equals a movement in space"—and in the course of finding a pictorial means of achieving the appropriate kind of space and the light that would permit its breathing, she invented a new medium which, beginning as a means to an end, turned out to be an end in itself.

Apart from drawings, up to 1928 and with one or two isolated examples in 1929 and 1930 watercolour was her primary method of producing the sketches on which to base her finished paintings. Watercolour, which she had learned to handle with such command in France, was nonetheless cumbersome, especially when it had to be handled in awkward locations and in the frequently poor weather conditions that were part of out-of-door practice. Moreover, watercolour lacks covering power; the colour slides and bleeds on the wet paper, and vigourous brushwork carrying its own movement is not possible.

A number of works in oil around 1929–30 indicate that her evolving expressive needs were demanding an alternative medium to watercolour; their freedom of handling and their exploratory character, changing from one moment to the next, declare their intention as sketches. They were done on paper board, card or paper. One of several carried out in a monochrome of blacks and greys is the vigorous untitled forest interior in the Vancouver Art Gallery's collection (42.3.56); its dense matrix of dark forms puts it still in her sombre mode, but the agitated angular movement of the foliage aligns it with the new governing

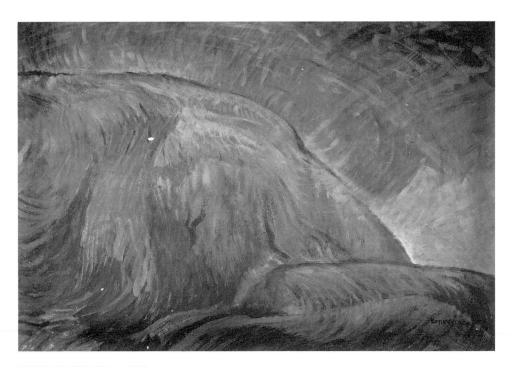

ROCKS BY THE SEA C.1939
Oil on paper, 59.7 x 86.36 cm
Location unknown

Untitled (forest interior,
black, grey, white) c.1930
Oil on paper, 88.2 x 60 cm
Vancouver Art Gallery, 42.3.56

Untitled (trees), brush drawing 1930–31 (left)
Oil and charcoal on paper, 45.9 x 29.7 cm
Vancouver Art Gallery, 42.3.170

ABOVE THE TREES C.1939
Oil on paper, 91.2 x 61 cm
Vancouver Art Gallery, 42.3.83

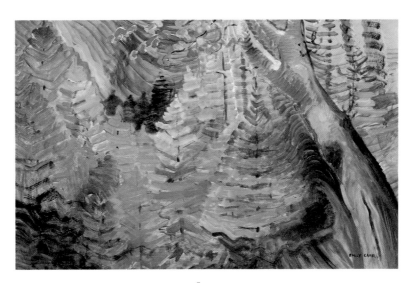

YOUNG PINES AND OLD MAPLE 1938
Oil on paper, 59.8 x 89.7 cm
Vancouver Art Gallery, 42.3.76

impulse to animation. There are other sketches of wooded interiors or tree studies done in full colour as well as some freely brushed drawings using dry black pigment on paper. Sometimes these sketches were thickly painted, and the sinking of the oil into the absorbent surfaces has left parched surfaces which inhibit the sense of fluid movement she was working towards. Like the charcoal drawings of Port Renfrew and the sketches in drawing books also done in 1929–30, they belong to that short period of intense search for formal means of expression; but this group was looking for new technical solutions as well. They can be seen as developing models for the oil-on-paper paintings which constitute such an important part of her work from 1932 on.

The technique she developed was simple and practical. Artists' materials were expensive then as now, and she was always short of money.[8] She bought quantities of inexpensive manila paper and ordinary white house paint to mix with her artist's colours, and by using a lot of thinner (gasoline) she had a fluid and quick-drying medium which could give her the transparency of watercolour without the problem of the colour floating or bleeding on the wet paper. Alternatively she could have the opacity and structuring capability of oil if she applied the paint thickly. She could now also use gestural movements of the brush as freely as she wanted. An immensely practical person, she devised a folding drawing board to which she could pin her full or half sheets of paper, and armed with that and her folding stool, easel and notebook she was equipped to go where her material beckoned. In a letter to the National Gallery's director, who had mistakenly referred to SKY, the sketch they had just purchased, as a watercolour, she described her new medium: "It is a kind of sketchy medium I have used for the last three or four years. Oil paint used thin with gasoline on paper. . . . It is inexpensive, light to carry and allows great freedom of thought and action. Woods and skies out west are big. You can't pin them down."[9]

Speaking in her Journals of her sketching experience she says:

Sketching in the big woods is wonderful. You go, find a space wide enough to sit in and clear enough so that the undergrowth is not drowning you. Then, being elderly, you spread your camp stool and sit and look around. 'Don't see much here. Wait.' Out comes the cigarette. The mosquitoes back away from the smoke.

Everything is green. Everything is waiting and still. Slowly things begin to move, to slip into their place. Groups and masses and lines tie themselves together. Colours you had not noticed come out, timidly or boldly. In and out, in and out your eye passes. Nothing is crowded; there is living space for all. Air moves between each leaf. Sunlight plays and dances. Nothing is still now. Life is sweeping through the spaces. Everything is alive. The air is alive. The silence is full of sound. The green is full of colour. Light and dark chase each other. Here is a picture, a complete thought, and there another and there. . . . There are themes everywhere, something sublime, something ridiculous , or joyous, or calm, or mysterious. Tender youthfulness laughing at gnarled oldness. Moss and ferns, and leaves and twigs, light and air, depth and colour chattering. . . . You must be still in order to hear and see.[10]

The use of the new medium coincided with the beginning of a fairly regulated pattern of work. Her raw material could be found close to home now that a search for native material no longer required her to go on long trips. Within reach of Victoria were opportunities for all the kinds of nature experiences that she would require for the rest of her painting life: the varied district of Metchosin, with its woods and jungle, its gentler rural spots, or its Albert Head's view of the sea; the deep cathedral-like interior of noble old trees preserved in the park at Goldstream Flats; Langford with its logged-off clearing and yellow moss-covered rocks; Cordova Bay with its prospect of both the Strait of Juan de Fuca and gentle farmland. And still at her back door was Beacon Hill Park with Dallas Road beach and cliffs, the source of many of her "sea and sky" paintings. Those and many others.

The sketching sessions in such locations, usually one in the spring and another in the fall or late summer—more if she could manage it—and lasting a couple of weeks or a month depending on weather and her health, became the pivot around which her work and her life revolved. On days when things went well she would do three or even four large sketches varying the pace at times with smaller sketches or drawings.[11] The rest of the year was spent working from the sketches, much of it longing for the next period of living and sketching in nature. "What I am after is out there in the woods—even the sketches to me are canned food. I like it fresh. Carry it right home and use it."[12]

The trips could be said to have commenced in May 1931 with a three-week stay in Cordova Bay, which resulted in a group of sketches whose strong, coarse graphic quality and prominent black pigment distinguish them from more painterly examples that familiarity with the medium soon produced. This trip was shared with a painting friend, as were two others,[13] but she preferred to be alone when working, enjoying visitors at other times and having "friends not too near and not too far." At first, and again later on, she rented a cottage or cabin; but in the summer of 1933 she purchased a small used van in which she, her pets and her equipment could be hauled by truck to accessible level sites near Victoria suitable to her diminishing agility but more than adequate for her sketching purposes. Only rarely do her sketches give any indication that habitation was sometimes very close to her location, which might be just around the corner from farm or other buildings, or that she was hidden from the road by only a screen of trees.

The sketches of the years 1933 to 1936 when she had the van are her most direct and free, and the times when she was living in it and working from it were surely the most blissful of her adult years. Life in the van was simple and also permitted the activities that mattered most to her. She had her animals and her best-loved books, and the domestic self in her that enjoyed homey things could contentedly improvise housekeeping arrangements. But most important of all, the barrier between herself and nature— "just a canvas and a rib or two and then the world"[14]—was so minimal as to be practically nonexistent, a situation which her work at that time neatly paraphrased. In June 1934, after a night of rain, she writes:

> Quite a downpour but what care we, snugged up all cosy under the old tin hen [that is, the van, usually referred to as "the elephant"]. The rain comes in insignificant little titters on the canvas top with an occasional heavy ha-ha-ha as the big accumulated drops roll off the pine boughs. Susie [her pet rat] cavorts round in glee and all the rest snore cosily. I am a lucky woman, I have a brick in a biscuit tin at my feet, and a lovely afternoon's writing before me, and the mystery of the solemn wood to look into. It's a very nice wood but wickedly full of mosquitoes. Perhaps they belong to the mystery. Doubtless they, with their poisonous little pricks, have their place and undoubtedly they

enjoy us. Three baby fir trees sit on the edge of the solemn wood and look as out of place as children at a grown-ups' party. Ghost flowers grow in the woods. I shall take a big clump home. They are mystery flowers.[15]

The oil-on-papers had their disadvantages. The fragility of the sketches was a concern for Carr and remained one for their early owners: the cheap manila paper she used is very brittle and soon deteriorates and cracks if not properly mounted. At first she mounted them on mosquito netting ("muslin" as she called it) in preparation for exhibiting and then later, when that proved unsatisfactory, soaked them off their netting backings and glued them on plywood. Unfortunately, the bonding agent in the plywood had a deleterious effect on the paper, and today most of them, at least those in public collections, have been mounted on a proper permanent and inert surface.

The yellow-browning of the paper as it has aged has altered the colour and tonal intention of the sketch, sometimes to the point that it is impossible to visualize what the original picture might have looked like. This, of course, is especially true when the wash of pigment was very thin and transparent and when large amounts of the paper were left uncovered. In several cases, sketches have been varnished, no doubt in the hope of conserving the work but with unfortunate visual results. On the other hand, occasionally the pervasive faded orange tint of the paper acts to unify an otherwise scattered composition.

There were other consequences that had to do with the paper, as she discovered. "Worked on some sketches that needed strengthening in expression. The paper will not take enough studied labour."[16] However carefully the idea for the sketch was thought out in advance, as her spontaneity increased the act of painting came out of the moment's swift feeling for it, something that cannot be maintained at will, and the fragile paper support did not allow for reworking. This problem relates, not unexpectedly, to the number of failed works in this medium, works where the tenuous bond between the idea and the brush, which had to move swiftly to capture the thought, broke down. The sketches served the purpose formerly filled by drawing; it was a proliferating method in which errors had to be expected as part of the process.

STUDY IN MOVEMENT 1935-36
Oil on canvas, 68.6 x 111.8 cm
Art Gallery of Ontario, Toronto

"At One with the Whole"

As the new paradigm asserted itself, the character of the natural world represented in the paintings changed completely. In the 1928–29 canvases, trees, poles, rocks, foliage—even skies—were visualized as well-defined, contained, very tangible sculpted forms: a solid and heavy world. Solidity and containment are on the side of immobility, and so Carr took the logical painter's steps leading to the dissolution of form. A sequence of paintings could be chosen, not necessarily following their true chronological order but illustrating a conceptual progression in which the solid matter of her forms becomes, through the transforming power of movement, soft and plastic and then deliquescent, finally vapourizing into air, light and space. Such a group might be: A YOUNG TREE, DEEP FOREST, STUDY IN MOVEMENT, ABOVE THE GRAVEL PIT and SKY. Specific forms in nature have progressively lost their defining edges, their particular substance, almost their identity, as they sway and merge in a mutual life of movement.

The brush stroke is the agent of the dissolution and the generator of movement within the new animated form. She found the means for realizing the full goal of her art while working within the oil-on-paper medium which she was then able to apply to canvas as well. "Freedom and *direction*" is something she learned from the medium, she said. "You are so unafraid to slash away because material scarcely counts. You use just can paint and there's no loss with failures."[17] Great sweeps of the arm could now be used as a means of capturing movement while the colour path of the brush retained its shape and direction without having to wait for the paper to dry. And so the strokes became forms of energy in themselves, units of direction, speed or strength, carrying whatever expressive value she intended for them. Working in the thin medium, the brush moves in easy waves across the paper from one side to the other in a continuous flow, uniting the foliage of a stand of trees in one fluid movement; it tracks the spiralling of branches revolving upwards in tilted whorls around a tree trunk; it punctures the sky and lets the dazzle through or curls it into spinning disks. When substantial areas of the paper are left untouched and the linear emphasis of the brush stroke is strong, the sketches read as coloured drawings. In one group the

SKY 1935–36
Oil on paper, 57.7 x 90.7 cm
National Gallery of Canada

ABOVE THE GRAVEL PIT 1937 (top)
Oil on canvas, 77.2 x 102.3 cm
Vancouver Art Gallery, 42.3.30

FOREST (tree trunks) 1938–39
Oil on paper, 90.8 x 60.3 cm
Private collection

TREE (spiralling upward) 1932–33
Oil on paper, 87.5 x 58 cm
Vancouver Art Gallery, 42.3.63

FOREST LANDSCAPE I 1939
Oil on paper, 91.5 x 61 cm
National Gallery of Canada

STUMPS AND SKY c.1934 (left)
Oil on paper, 59.5 x 90 cm
Vancouver Art Gallery, 42.3.66

HAPPINESS 1939
Oil on paper, 84.8 x 54 cm
Private collection

gestural brush takes off on its own with hardly more than a glancing reference to trees or ground swell or cloud as the particulars of nature are absorbed into the brush's compulsive energy.

With the reinstatement of the visible brush stroke as the chief pictorial means, light is also assigned a new role. No longer used dramatically as illumination reflected *on* the surfaces of forms, or descending in articulated shafts, light now simply fills the picture, dimly or brightly as the case demands. This is accomplished through the transparency of the diluted oil colour, which allows the white of the paper to reflect light back through, and by her handling of the loaded brush, somewhat like an oriental calligrapher, varying the density of the colour within the stroke as it moves and throwing off a breathing, modulated light that changes according to the path it takes.

As a corollary to such changes, a degree of the painterly immediacy that her French-influenced work possessed is now restored to her work, a quality which the sculptured formal concept of her 1928–31 canvases had denied. Again, excepting the period of her "French" paintings Carr was not a colourist; she did not, for instance, compose or structure in colour as Cézanne did, though even in her formal period she had her earthy generic green or green-brown as Harris had his rarefied blue. But in these last ten years of painting, colour assumes a larger role not only as space opens up into blue sky and light illuminates a more varied world of nature but also as the painted *tache* (now become linear) drops its subservience to modelled form.

The new medium also helped her replace an earlier static principle of spatial composition in which layers of forms were marshalled behind one another like wings on a stage moving back from the picture surface. In observation of the common convention of foreground, middle ground and distant space, it had been her frequent habit in the 1928–31 canvases to separate the imagined space of the picture from the actual space of the spectator by some strong compositional feature thrust into the foreground: a rock, a log, a hillock. Occasionally this feature appeared contrived, an artificial space filler. The habit lingers on to weaken some of the later works, but once under the spell of "continuous movement" Carr is often able to dispense with this device. The strongest, most daring paintings are those in which the composi-

Untitled (Clover Point from
Dallas Road Beach, Victoria) 1935–36
Oil on paper, 57.2 x 86.4 cm
Private collection

SWIRL 1937 (top)
Oil on canvas, 68.3 x 57.8 cm
Private collection

tion is not framed by forms that restate the picture's margins but rather those in which the animating movement of a picture sweeps up and into and through its space without hindrance. In such works the picture space is simply part of the infinite space that by implication continues in all directions in and out and beyond the frame. Many of the paintings now cease to have a central focus in the traditional way of composing inherited from the Renaissance, as forms abandon hierarchic character to join the compulsive flow of energy. Even in cases where there is nominally a central feature, such as a single tree, it turns out that the sky, or the rhythm created by wind sweeping all the parts into its dominance, is really the subject.

The habit persists of referring to Carr's oil-on-paper works as sketches, a term referring conventionally to works preparatory to the more important—because more carefully worked out— canvases. She herself called them sketches and that was their original intention. But so suited was the medium to the purposes of her work during the late years and so liberating to her genius that many achieved a completeness of realization which makes them comparable to the best of her canvases. Some were touched up, some led to canvases or other sketches, and some remain as free sketchy drawings in paint. Together they must be considered a major body of her work among which are many of her most daring and unique efforts.

Despite the obvious speed with which the oil-on-papers were executed, sketching for her was not simply a matter of dashing off excited sensations or collecting visual information; it required sitting down and quietly, thoughtfully allowing a pictorial idea to sort itself out of nature's jumble. Lawren Harris had suggested the usefulness of jotting down ideas, and a notebook in which to clarify her ideas in words became part of the regular equipment accompanying her sketching expeditions.

After 1931, once she was using this medium, the conceptual distinction between preliminary study and canvas became blurred since the sketch took on the task of the main conceptual search as well as the immediate impression. Both sketch and canvas then were products of essentially the same intent, and the difference between them was one largely of fuller development and fine-tuning of relationships in the richer and more durable medium.

YOUNG AND OLD FOREST 1936
Oil on paper, 91.4 x 60.3 cm
Edmonton Art Gallery
Gift of Dr. and Mrs. Max Stern

SOMETHING UNNAMED 1937
Oil on canvas, 112.2 x 68.9 cm
Private collection

The unity of vision that evolved between the two phases of work is witnessed in such a pair as the canvas SOMETHING UNNAMED and the related sketch YOUNG AND OLD FOREST.

Early works in the paper medium tended to be relatively formal and stiff with discrete forms and perhaps centred compositions. Spontaneity in execution increased keeping pace with a concept that centred on movement, and spontaneity also became a developing characteristic in the canvases. The problem of maintaining the immediacy and fervour of the sketch in the canvas—one familiar to artists working in the landscape tradition—was not serious for her, even though she continued to lament it; and in a few late canvases it virtually disappeared. In SOMBRENESS SUNLIT the gestural brush almost takes over from the conceptualizing mind, as it sometimes does in the sketches, and the canvas too seems to come out of the act of painting itself. The success of such canvases depends on retaining the brush's direct connection with the initiating impulse, as it also does in the sketch; but in the canvas it had to be maintained in the denser, less fluid—and inhibitingly expensive—medium.

At this time Carr's confidence was high, her main creative hurdles past, and notions of the ongoingness of things were dominating her art and her thinking. "I want [my paintings]. . . [to] not sit down anywhere en route. . . . I want to express growing, not stopping, being still on the move."[18] It is in keeping with this attitude that her production (not speaking of temporal interruptions due to illness after 1937) was characterized stylistically and qualitatively by steady even flow rather than peaks and hollows. Nonetheless, there are a number of authoritative canvases which stand out like paradigmatic markers in the particular eddies of energy that swirl around them. They would include among others REFORESTATION, WOOD INTERIOR, FIR TREE AND SKY, SCORNED AS TIMBER, BELOVED OF THE SKY, and SHORELINE.

For those who must classify, the prolific output of Carr's last and climactic years presents its own mix of reward and challenge. She always started with real places and specific information no matter what broader import she extracted from them, and so many of the sketches (and their related canvases) show identifiable topographical features by which they can be located geographically: the gravel pits of Metchosin, the logged-off terrain of

SOMBRENESS SUNLIT 1938–40
Oil on canvas, 111.9 x 68.6 cm
British Columbia Archives PDP 633

REFORESTATION d.1936
Oil on canvas, 110 x 67.2 cm
McMichael Canadian Art Collection,
Kleinburg, Ont.

DANCING SUNLIGHT 1939–40
Oil on canvas, 83.5 x 60 cm
McMichael Canadian Art Collection,
Kleinburg, Ont.

FIR TREE AND SKY 1935–36
Oil on canvas, 102 x 69 cm
National Gallery of Canada
Bequest of Mrs. J. P. Barwick
(from the Douglas M. Duncan Collection)

METCHOSIN 1934–35
Oil on paper, 87.6 x 57.2 cm
Private collection

Langford, the ancient cedars of Goldstream Park and others. Then too she often developed an identifying set of visual signs during the course of a sketching session in response to the character and mood of a particular location, such as the circular disks in sunny blue skies that characterize paintings done during her September 1935 sketching session at Albert Head in Metchosin. By putting together information from such observations with that from her Journals, and the detailed chronicling of the sketching trips as to place and date that now exists,[19] a framework of chronology and geography emerges by which a good many of the works can be located. There remain, however, a number of them, especially those that stem from more generalized subject material—the ubiquitous trees, undergrowth, forest edge and so on—that resist such classification. Carr herself had little patience with the taxonomic efforts of historians or curators once the specificity of everything except the precise perceived idea for each painting had ceased to matter to her.

Grouping the works thematically according to the kind of nature they deal with comes closer to Carr's intention for them: sky, sea and sky, jungle, young "dancing" trees, wooded interior, field at the edge of woods, and so on. But if we are interested in the full dimension of what she was reaching for we should go in search of her painting-thoughts or painting-ideas. For as she said in a letter to a friend, speaking of the need to meditate on her summer's work: "I like to find definitely what my summer's work was about before trying to 'canvas.' You are generally I find, going for some specific thing. . . ."[20]

Carr was well aware of the truth fundamental to art as it was practised and still understood in her day, that any single work must be based on one central idea within which all aspects of the picture's making—colour, handling, composition, scale—find their character: "Do not try to do extraordinary things but do ordinary things with intensity. Push your idea to the limit, distorting if necessary to drive the point home and intensify it, but stick to the one central idea, getting it across at all costs. Have a central idea in any picture and let all else in the picture lead up to that one thought or idea. Find the leading rhythm and the dominant style or predominating form. Watch negative and positive colour."[21]

The "thought," the "idea," the "theme," "the vital thing."
Throughout the Journals, and especially in their record of the
early years when she is consolidating her new authority, she
comes to this notion again and again, imprinting it on her consciousness in words. The theme—or her "thought" in the full
meaning she gave the word—was not a factor in her work before
1928, or it was so only in the degree to which the imagination of
the innate artist imposes its poetry on its material involuntarily.
In her early days she was painting "subjects" in the conventional
sense, the facts of nature: the trees, the cliff, the beachdrift. But
Carr is now the aware artist working out of more layers of her
psyche and experience.

The "thought" whose emergence she awaits when she goes
sketching is multidimensional, and in the following passage she
pursues one such particular thought:

> I am painting a flat landscape, low-lying hills with an expanding
> sky. What am I after—crush and exaltation? It is not a landscape
> and not sky but something outside and beyond the enclosed
> forms. I grasp for a thing and a place one cannot see with these
> eyes, only very very faintly with one's higher eyes. I begin to see
> that everything is perfectly balanced so that what one borrows one
> must pay back in some form or another, that everything has its
> own place but is interdependent on the rest, that a picture, like
> life, must also have perfect balance. Every part of it also is depen-
> dent on the whole and the whole is dependent on every part. It is a
> swinging rhythm of thought, swaying back and forth, leading up
> to, suggesting, waiting, urging the unordered statement to come
> forth and proclaim itself, voicing the notes from its very soul to be
> caught up and echoed by other souls, filling space and at the same
> time leaving space, shouting but silent. Oh, to be still enough to
> hear and see and know the glory of the sky and earth and sea![22]

We do not know which particular painting she was referring to,
but the passage reveals various aspects of her "thought" and
hence her intent. There is the swift grasp of the physical character
and expressive nature of the place: the flatness, the low-lying
hills, the expanding sky—and the overall expressive communication of "crush and exaltation." The thought is also simultaneously "seen" in its pictorial terms, and in this period of her art
that means in terms of movement in the picture-space. The
rhythm here is a swinging one, "swaying back and forth" and

"leading up." Behind everything, of course, qualifying all nature, including this individual experience of it, is the sublime encompassing thought: "the glory of the sky and earth and sea!"

Carr the knowledgeable picture maker, finding form equivalents for what her eye saw, handling positive-negative relationships, balancing rhythms, can be taken for granted an astonishingly large proportion of the time considering the freer structure of her work after 1931. Even in occasional flawed paintings where a form is unaccounted for or a colour has gone soggy, the expressive force is strong enough to compel our admiring attention. It is the nature of the expressive content that interests us in the present context, however. She is totally in her art at this time, nothing essential in her psychic or emotional life held back, and she has instinctively uncovered, through her painting, contents in the natural world that correspond with states of feeling and being buried within the human psyche. That connection is expressed in art through elements that are at every painter's disposal, and Carr was now using them for that purpose. Thought of in this light, the significance of specific geographic locations or of natural features in her work diminishes as she layers it with other levels of content: that is to say, the path-through-Armadale-woods (or some other woods) becomes also the generic path-through-woods, to become the numinous and paradigmatic path-through.

Particular sketching places become then the sites for certain elemental experiences which she explores again and again in her art in all their variations. The experience of *space*: as in the silent, hollow deep in the enclosing forest, or scooped out in great sucking hollows in cliffsides or gravel pits, or lifting out and up into tree tops or endless skies. ("I find that raising my eyes slightly above what I am regarding so that the thing is a little out of focus seems to bring the spiritual into clearer vision, as though there were something lifting the material up to the spiritual.")[23] There was her preoccupation with *movement* (her indicator of life and the agent for symbolizing its presence), movement as in the windswept branches or as the crawl and relentless spread of undergrowth. There was her grasp of *light* with its potential to reveal and its promise of life, and its disquieting absence, dark.

It could be noted that when in her maturity Carr was able to find within herself such deep identification with the very process

SUNSHINE AND TUMULT 1938–39
Oil on paper, 87 x 57.1 cm
Art Gallery of Hamilton,
bequest of H. S. Southam

of nature, she "transcended the personal" as Harris had once recommended. Her natural tendency to endow all things with some
kind of life shows in her writing in the form of homey metaphor:
the sketching caravan that was named the "elephant" and then as
familiarity set in was sometimes referred to as the "old hen," and
so on. The discrete forms of nature she used in the earlier paintings of this last period sometimes became adversely infected by
this same impulse. For instance, in paintings dealing with the
cycle of life, a frequent theme, she might risk casting her forms in
obvious roles such as the young, dancing, joyous tree performing
on stage surrounded by sober and sympathetic elders. But any
inclination to subjective interpretation disappeared once she perceived nature in its broadest terms as simply the continuing process of creation, an oceanic world of continuous ebb and change,
with nature's particular manifestations and herself as part of them
swept up into its larger life. The-cycle-of-life theme then is trans-
lated into the enormous pervasive sexual energy of her painting as
openings and enclosures vibrate with light and movement, trunks
thrust upward into sky, earth fecundates, and death and decay are
assimilated into the irresistible regenerative cycle.

When she feels the expressive potential of each of such primal
energies at their most intense we get works of striking power. In
SCORNED AS TIMBER, BELOVED OF THE SKY radiant, light-filled
space realized as feathered and lightly undulating strokings of
pigment makes a firmament of the sky in a statement of transcendence and ecstatic unification with all of creation. In the sketch
CHILL DAY IN JUNE and in FOREST the nervous energy in the cal-
ligraphic line of the brush seems a force on its own, a compulsive
cosmic blip lodged in the maker's hand or eye—or psyche. In the
restless organic life that permeates works like the latter we find
spiritual affinities for Carr with other natural expressionists
throughout history—Grünewald, El Greco or some of the
northern illuminators of early Gothic manuscripts—though
without their frequent overtone of nerve-edge excitation.

As life in the modern world distances us farther and farther
from meaningful contact with sources of primal energy, such
ways of making and thinking about art have become outmoded.
In fact, today they are largely unimaginable to generations who
have grown up in a cultural climate so different in fundamental

WOOD INTERIOR 1932–35
Oil on canvas, 130 x 86.3 cm
Vancouver Art Gallery, 42.3.5

ROOTS 1937–39
Oil on canvas, 112 x 69 cm
British Columbia Archives PDP 635

SCORNED AS TIMBER, BELOVED OF THE SKY 1935
Oil on canvas, 112 x 68.9 cm
Vancouver Art Gallery, 42.3.15

CHILL DAY IN JUNE 1938–39
Oil on paper, 106 x 75 cm
Maltwood Art Museum and Gallery,
University of Victoria

SEASCAPE C.1936
Oil on paper, 57 x 85.2 cm
Private collection

ways from that of Carr's time. Not only has painting moved from its central place to the margins of the visual arts spectrum but, aestheticism having run its course as the central faith of modernism, it has also lost its painterly visibility. Painting, including painting of the past, is today *read* (as a set of cognitive references) rather than *seen* (as autonomous pictorial signs), *interpreted* rather than *felt*.

But those older ways and attitudes, though already being left behind by more advanced artists, were still abroad in Carr's day and they carried over what was essentially a religious belief in the expressive nature and purpose of art as vested in the personal vision and power of the individual artist. In her time, moreover, the continued existence of the natural world to which her art was anchored, was an assumption still beyond questioning. What distinguishes her among others of her era and faith is the intensity of her vision and the extent to which she was able to push the painter's basic elements to the edges of their understood practice and significance, to uncover content in nature that resonated with basic human feelings and states of being. It was at this level of perception that the wonder and mystery set in and the connection with the "serene throb" that Carr yearned to make was accomplished.

In 1942, three years before her death, Carr returned in several paintings to themes that had preoccupied her ten or twelve years before, restating them within the context of dominant movement but in a mood of lyrical tranquility rather than intense energy. She chose one last time to enter the dark world of forest interior in QUIET and CEDAR where we have again the enclosing wall of green forest set close against the picture surface, stretching edge to edge, no sky above, no anchoring earth below, no deep space leading us in. Unlike their earlier prototypes, these are tapestrylike in their soft flatness, projecting a mood of serenity and rest in which forms are relaxed and rhythms fall gently.

The resurfacing of the Indian theme was discussed in the previous section, but it does not seem inappropriate to include the 1942 SKIDEGATE POLE here, for in it Carr's two streams of inspiration come together at the end of her painting life, again in balance as they had been for a short while in 1930–31. Comparing it with the 1912 canvas of the same subject, on which it is

QUIET d.1942
Oil on canvas, 111.76 x 68.58 cm
Private collection

CEDAR d.1942
Oil on canvas, 112 x 69 cm
Vancouver Art Gallery, 42.3.28

A SKIDEGATE POLE 1941–42
Oil on canvas, 87 x 76.5 cm
Vancouver Art Gallery, 42.3.37

closely based, we see it as one of those large works summarizing and synthesizing much of what has gone before in a statement that also represents a new position. The flat art nouveau patterns of sky and trees form a decorative background to the pole in the early painting whereas in the late version nature becomes an ambient environment of light and movement whose space and life, so to speak, the pole shares. The sea of growth and the whirl of sky are made of the same substance, differentiated only by luminous colour which embraces the Indian form in the glow of its damped–down brilliance. The early picture had a pictorial unity; the late painting tells of other unities as well.

Afterword

Author Margaret Atwood's probe into the nature of the "Canadian-ness" of Canadian literature in her seminal book *Survival*[1] is frequently summoned by writers seeking to understand the problems faced by Carr and other Canadian artists. In her analysis Atwood saw a young country without traditions of its own, whose colonial origins hung heavily over it, naturally invoking old-world cultural models which did not fit the experience of the vast, rugged and sparsely populated New World. While the Old World continued until recently to view Canadian cultural products with imperial condescension, if at all, Canada itself for complex demographic, political and social reasons failed to produce a society that could provide within it the integral and assumed place for its artists without which they might be expected to perish, to survive crippled, or to turn out products marked by their peculiar struggle. Victoria and British Columbia were but part of a common Canadian condition, even though it was exaggerated there by geographic distancing and a late entry into the field. At the time Carr was maturing it is doubtful that any city in Canada except Toronto or Montreal could have provided a sufficient audience to convince its artists—especially women artists—that they were being taken seriously as contributing members of society.

Looked at as a whole the striking thing about Carr's career is its late flowering and the few years in which she produced her major work relative to the whole long course of her art activity. Those paintings which have become lodged in the imagination of Canadians and a slowly increasing number of people in other countries were done after she was in her fifty-eighth year in the little more than a decade of active painting remaining to her. It was only then that she emerged a survivor from her artist's struggle—a major figure, whole though a little scarred—to produce a body of work whose vitality reflected as much of life's light as dark, and which effectively demonstrated that art of great strength and conspicuous individuality could be produced in a remote corner of the country if the artist had the necessary qualities and a little bit of luck.

The sheer strength of her character and of her vision, once she found her centre, were sufficient to see her through the absence—or later distance—of an effective audience, as well as through other problems. Her bond with the part of the world she grew up in was an unshakeable certainty: "This is my country. What I want to express is *here* and I love it. Amen!"[2] That core of certainty was based on an intense experience of nature; and, unlike the experience of city-bred European immigrants when confronted with the sternness of Canadian nature, hers was rooted in the total sensory experience of a benign childhood involving her senses of touch and smell as much as her eyes. She had as well, apparently from the beginning, the inborn wisdom to reject the values of a conventional society that would not have permitted the fierce artist in her to emerge. As it was she did inherit enough of those values to make the going difficult and to retard the attainment of her full powers.

When it came to the problem of how to relate to the artistic models and language from which she needed to learn, given her isolation in the Far West, her utter sureness of who she was, her high intelligence, and her aversion to intellectualization stood her in good stead. She absorbed the lessons of French Post-Impressionism, a modern international approach to painting that had not yet been imported to her part of the country, with excited ease, enabling her to cast off the last residue of Victorian painting attitudes. Her slow recognition that the liberating new style did not fully engage the character of her own cultural experience failed to shake her attachment to her place but simply delayed the process of artistic self-discovery. Cubism as a means of giving structure to her painting, though it occupied but a brief place in her work, was critical in enabling her to shift her art to the symbolic mode in which she "found" herself, first in dark Indian-dominated canvases and then in transcendental nature paintings. Her intuitive sense of her own needs enabled her to interpret and adapt such modernist international movements to her own Canadian West Coast vision without becoming enmeshed in their historical or theoretical aspects. She was fortunate in being able to take from them what was relevant to her purpose while remaining in the best sense an innocent.

In attitude Carr relates strongly to European and American nineteenth-century nature Romanticism: to Wordsworth's rapture in all natural things and to Whitman's full sensuous embrace of the universe. However ambitious her aspiration to touch universal chords of creative resonance through her work, she was able to avoid banality because her faith, like Whitman's, and her practice were grounded in real places and particular experiences of nature. She relates also to the spirit of northern European symbolism through the medium of the Group of Seven. There is an occasional startling parallel between some of her nature paintings and those of Edvard Munch of 1903–04. At the same time her specific pictorial connection with Post-Impressionist art and with Cubism link her to the predominant aesthetic concerns of the broad modernist current of the twentieth century. Her strong individualism and her spirit of innovation are qualities she shares with a host of artists of her time with whose work her own sometimes shows a kinship, though she saw it briefly or not at all; thus, for instance, the pervasive sexual component in her painting parallels that in the work of Georgia O'Keeffe. Here, as so often with Carr, affinities with other artists are more a matter of unconsciously related goals than of stylistic similarity. She herself, following the banner of the Group of Seven, wanted her art to be emphatically "Canadian," something she could accomplish (as she was able to rationalize) by painting out of her long-sustained devotion to the Canadian West Coast. And British Columbian and Canadian her art undoubtedly is. But in reaching so unreservedly into the well of her emotional and spiritual resources, she transcended her Canadianism to join a company of individuals—mystic artists who are not necessarily connected by nationality or time. Their numbers would include such names as Lawren Harris and Mark Tobey as well as Samuel Palmer and Arthur Dove, and even William Blake whom she admired—artists whose work hers little resembles, but who also trapped something of the "glows and glories" that emanate from the world of ordinary reality.

Chronology

1871 Born Victoria, 12 December 1871, of English parents, same year British Columbia became a Province of the Dominion of Canada.

1879–87 Takes art lessons while attending Mrs. Fraser's Private School; then attends Central Public School. Mother dies, 1886.

1888 Father dies, leaving trust fund for his six living children. Enrolls in Victoria High School but leaves after a year. Continues private art lessons.

1890–93 Secures guardian's permission to enroll in California School of Design, San Francisco. Studies drawing, portraiture, still life and landscape.

1893–95 Returns to Victoria; holds art classes for children in converted loft of family barn. Receives prize for drawings at annual agricultural fair in 1894 and 1895.

1899 Visits Nootka Indian reserve at Ucluelet, west coast of Vancouver Island and is given name Klee Wyck ("laughing one") by natives. Meets William Locke Paddon, a persistent but finally unsuccessful suitor. Leaves for England in August and enrolls at London's Westminster School of Art. Approaches Beatrix Potter's publisher with her Ucluelet sketches but is turned down.

1900–03 Finds London unsympathetic but works more happily in locations away from the city: in Berkshire, Cornwall (studying with Julius Olsson and Algernon Talmage) and Hertfordshire (with watercolourist John Whiteley). Enters East Anglia Sanatorium, Suffolk, in January after repeated breakdowns in health.

1904 Leaves Sanatorium in March after eighteen-month stay and returns to Whiteley's classes. Leaves for Canada in June. Stops in Toronto and Cariboo district of British Columbia before returning to Victoria in October.

1905 Produces political cartoons for Victoria's *The Week*.

1906 Moves to Vancouver where she will live until summer of 1910; rents studio at 570 Granville Street and teaches at Vancouver Studio Club (VSC) and School of Art. Exhibits with VSC's first annual. Makes lifelong friend of Sophie Frank, basket maker of North Vancouver native reserve.

1907   Travels with sister Alice to Alaska, sees monumental native carving for first time. Resolves to document dying heritage of natives. Wins one of four purchase prizes in vsc exhibition. Continues teaching private classes in Vancouver. Sketching locations include Stanley Park.

1908–09   Becomes founding member of British Columbia Society of Fine Arts (BCSFA). Exhibits with BCSFA as she will continue to do for most of her career. (From 1911–37 will also show regularly with the Island Arts and Crafts Society in Victoria.) Makes summer trips to Alert Bay, Campbell River and other southern Kwakiutl Indian villages; sketches at nearby reserves, Sechelt and North Vancouver as well as in Vancouver's Stanley Park. Teaches at Crofton House School for Girls, Vancouver.

1910   Holds studio show and auctions some work to raise money for trip to France. Leaves for France 11 July with sister Alice via Quebec and Liverpool. In Paris, meets English painter Harry Phelan Gibb and wife who introduce her to modern French painting. Enters classes at Académie Colarossi but finds private study with Scotsman Duncan Fergusson more profitable. Leaves his atelier in December because of ill health.

1911   Recuperates in Sweden. In France follows the Gibbs to Crécy-en-Brie and then to St. Efflam in northern Brittany. Goes to Concarneau and works in watercolour under New Zealand painter Frances Hodgkins. Has two paintings hung in Salon d'Automne exhibition in Paris. Returns to Victoria in November.

1912   Back in Vancouver, holds exhibition of French painting in her studio at 1465 W. Broadway in March. In July, sets out for ambitious six-week trip to native sites in coastal and central northern British Columbia, including Alert Bay area, Skeena River valley and Queen Charlotte Islands. Produces large number of drawings and paintings.

1913   Mounts large exhibit of accumulated Indian work hoping to sell her collection to the provincial government; offer declined. Returns to Victoria and builds small apartment house with revenue suites at 646 Simcoe St.

1914–27   Preoccupied with earning a living, paints only occasionally. Hooks rugs and makes pottery with Indian designs, raises dogs, sells fruit, attends to tenants and boarders. Spends eight months in San Francisco painting ballroom decorations for Hotel St. Francis. Draws series of cartoons for a feminist periodical. Her work attracts attention of Dr. Charles F. Newcombe and ethnologist C. Marius Barbeau, important future supporters. Painting and exhibiting activity increase somewhat after 1924 when she makes contact with several Seattle painters including Mark Tobey. Enrolls in correspondence course in short fiction.

1927   Pivotal year. Is visited by Barbeau and Eric Brown, director of National Gallery of Canada, who choose work for inclusion in historic exhibition in Ottawa of Canadian West Coast art. On trip east to attend opening in

November she meets members of the Group of Seven in Toronto, sees their work, begins sustaining friendship with Lawren Harris and artistic connection with eastern Canada.

1928   National Gallery purchases three watercolours. On return home resumes full painting activity, concentrating on Indian themes. Makes second ambitious trip to northern Indian sites: Alert Bay, Skeena and Nass valleys, Queen Charlotte Islands. September, American artist Mark Tobey gives class in Carr's studio and effects major change in her art.

1929   In active correspondence with Harris, commences period of spiritual search. Investigates Theosophy. Continues participation in local and regional exhibitions while commencing to be included in major national venues in eastern Canada and the United States, and occasionally abroad. Makes sketching trips to west coast of Vancouver Island and Port Renfrew.

1930–31   Spring of 1930, visits Toronto, Ottawa and New York. In August, makes final trip to Indian sites on Vancouver Island. Begins emphasizing nature themes in painting and commences pattern of spring and summer sketching expeditions to locations near Victoria. Winter 1931, works on portraits.

1932–33   Travels to Toronto (last time) and to Chicago World's Fair; misses art exhibit but sees and admires work by William Blake at Art Institute. Travels to provincial interior and paints mountainous country. Purchases a trailer which serves as sketching base for four summers. Becomes member of Canadian Group of Painters.

1934–35   Active sketching outdoors, painting and exhibiting. Gives talk at Provincial Normal School.

1936   Gives up Simcoe Street house, moves to 316 Beckley Street.

1937   Suffers angina attack. Writing temporarily replaces painting during recovery. Visited by Eric Newton.

1938–39   October 1938, has first of annual solo exhibits at Vancouver Art Gallery. Several works shown at Tate Gallery, London, which attract critical attention. Has serious heart attack. Stories introduced to Ira Dilworth who will become her editor and eventually literary executor of her estate.

1940   Moves in with Alice at 218 St. Andrew's Street. Her stories are read on CBC radio.

1941   Her first book *Klee Wyck* published, subsequently wins Governor General's award for non-fiction. Emily Carr Trust created establishing a permanent collection of her painting for the Province of B.C.

1942–43   Her last sketching trip, summer 1942. From now on spends much time in hospital or nursing home. *Book of Small* published. Has major exhibition at the Art Gallery of Toronto.

1945   *House of All Sorts* published. Dominion Gallery, Montreal, shows 59 works of which many are sold. Major works purchased by various galleries. Names Harris, Newcombe and Dilworth as trustees of her estate. Dies 2 March. Buried in Ross Bay Cemetery, Victoria.

Chapter Notes

The Background

1 Margaret Ormsby, "A Horizontal View," read before the Canadian Historical Association, Sherbrooke, P.Q., 9 June 1966, 11.

2 Small is the name of Carr's book about her childhood, and the name she used again in letters in later life to refer to the imaginative free child-spirit that persisted in the adult.

3 Carr wrote that her father "insisted on bringing his English big tin oven on legs around the 'Horn' as well as heavy mahogany furniture and the big pewter hot-water dishes that he ate his chops and steaks off." *The Book of Small,* 6.

4 Emily Carr, *Growing Pains,* 14.

5 Emily Carr, "Modern and Indian Art of the West Coast" in *Supplement to the McGill News* (June 1929), 20.

6 Emily Carr, *The Book of Small,* 96.

7 Carr to National Gallery Director Eric Brown, 1939, National Gallery of Canada. (Hereafter National Gallery.)

8 Carr, *Growing Pains,* 274.

9 Carr to Brown, Fall 1934, National Gallery.

10 Paula Blanchard, *The Life of Emily Carr,* 144: "[*The House of All Sorts*] like all her writing, is best read as a record of feeling rather than a narrative of fact."

11 Emily Carr, *Hundreds and Thousands,* 206.

12 Carr to Dilworth, 1941–42, British Columbia Archives and Records Service (hereafter BCARS).

Becoming an Artist; Becoming Carr

1 Carr, *Growing Pains,* 46–47.

2 Ibid., 26.

3 Ibid., 49.

4 Ibid., 73.

5 Ibid., 154.

6 Ibid., 157.

7 Ibid., 176.

8 Ibid., 181.

9 Ibid., 215.

10 Ibid., 216.

11 Hodgkins had been in Concarneau for the past two years. See Maria

Tippett, *Emily Carr: A Biography*, 93, who says that her summer classes were over when Carr arrived and that she was probably the only student working with Hodgkins.

12 The two entries in the catalogue were numbers 245 and 246, LA COLLINE and LE PAYSAGE. According to Blanchard (*The Life of Emily Carr*, 121) Gibb entered her paintings and Fergusson was on the jury.

13 Dennis Reid, *A Concise History of Canadian Painting*, 158.

14 Carr, *Growing Pains*, 232.

15 Ibid., 232.

16 Ibid., 237

17 Carr, *Hundreds and Thousands*, 8.

18 Jackson's statement is recorded by Roald Nasgaard in *The Mystic North: Symbolist Landscape Painting in Northern Europe and North America 1890–1940*, 159.

The Formation of a Mature Style

1 Written notes in a drawing book dated Dec. [1927], BCARS.

2 Carr, *Hundreds and Thousands*, 15.

3 Ibid., 17.

4 The painting referred to by Carr is almost certainly one of Harris's Lake Superior canvases and not a "sea painting."

5 Carr, *Hundreds and Thousands*, 15.

6 Carr, *Growing Pains*, 240.

7 William C. Seitz, *Mark Tobey*, 47.

8 Carr to Eric Brown, 1928, National Gallery.

9 Carr, *Hundreds and Thousands*, 21.

10 Colin Graham to Donald Buchanan, 19 July 1957, National Gallery.

11 Mark Tobey to Donald Buchanan, 15 April 1957, National Gallery.

12 Mark Tobey in an interview with Audrey St. D. Johnson, *Victoria Times*, 25 March 1957.

13 Mark Tobey to Donald Buchanan, 25 March 1957, National Gallery.

14 Carr's original journals, vol. 5, 4 April 1934, BCARS.

15 Tobey's reference to "Leonardo's discoveries" is also relevant here. I am indebted to Gerta Moray, who has made a study of Carr's 1928 paintings and whose doctoral thesis on Carr's Indian work is in progress, for drawing my attention to the precise chronological position and significance of Kitwancool Totems in this context.

16 Nasgaard, *The Mystic North*, 197.

17 Ruth Appelhof, *The Expressionist Landscape*, 72.

18 Doris Shadbolt, *The Art of Emily Carr*, 72.

19 Seitz, 46–47.

20 New York: Dial Press, 1928.

21 Appelhof, 60.

22 Pearson, 54.

23 Ibid., 122n.

24 Harris to Carr, undated (c. 1929), BCARS.

25 Pearson, fig. 27; reproduction of original etching by Pearson.

26 Pearson quoting words "borrowed from a friend" in a caption for figs. 57–60.

27 Carr, *Growing Pains*, 248.

28 Ibid., 250.

29 WOOD INTERIOR, collection Robert McLaughlin Gallery, Oshawa, Ontario.

An Interior Evolution: Belief and Attitudes

1   Maurice Tuchman, quoting from an interview with Richard Poussette-Dart in *The Spiritual in Art: Abstract Painting 1890–1950* (Los Angeles County Museum of Art, 1986), 18.

2   Carr, *Hundreds and Thousands*, 329.

3   Carr, *Growing Pains*, 15.

4   Carr, *Hundreds and Thousands*, 329.

5   Bertram Brooker, ed., *Yearbook of the Arts in Canada 1928–29*, 17.

6   Frederick Housser, *A Canadian Art Movement: The Story of the Group of Seven*, 215.

7   Housser, "Some Thoughts on National Consciousness," in the *Canadian Theosophist*, vol. 8, no. 5 (15 July 1927).

8   Housser, *A Canadian Art Movement*, 15.

9   Carr, *Hundreds and Thousands*, 8.

10 Ibid., 17.

11 Ibid., 19.

12 Ibid., 18.

13 Ibid., 21.

14 Ibid., 94.

15 Ibid., 93.

16 Ibid., 123.

17 Ibid., 42.

18 Harris to Carr, undated (c. 1929), BCARS.

19 Harris to Carr, 30 March 1932, BCARS.

20 Carr, *Hundreds and Thousands*, 123.

21 Harris to Carr, undated (c. 1929), BCARS.

22 Harris to Carr, 1930, BCARS.

23 Carr, *Hundreds and Thousands*, 3,4. An exception should be noted: two brief passages suggesting her innate spiritual nature were written on the trip to eastern Canada on 10 November 1927.

24 Tuchman, *The Spiritual in Art*, 65; see also Linda Street, "Emily Carr: Contact with Lawren Harris and Central Canada," Master's thesis, Carleton University, Ottawa, 1979, 20.

25 Carr, *Hundreds and Thousands*, 115.

26 Ibid., 30–31.

27 Ibid., 112.

28 Carr to Cheney, Cheney Papers, Dec. 1940, Special Collections, UBC Library.
29 Carr to Dilworth, Feb. (probably 1941), BCARS.
30 Pearson, *How to See Modern Pictures,* 92–93.
31 Emily Carr, *Fresh Seeing: Two Addresses by Emily Carr,* 12.
32 Carr's typed notes, undated, BCARS.
33 Kathleen Dreier, *Western Art and the New Era,* 74.
34 Ibid., 19.
35 Ibid., 12.
36 Carr, *Hundreds and Thousands,* 301.
37 Harris joined the Transcendental Painting Group in Taos, New Mexico, for a time in 1938.
38 Tuchman, 43.
39 See *Hundreds and Thousands,* 75, "Blake knew how!" She had gone to Chicago to see the art exhibition at the World's Fair but unfortunately arrived after the exhibition had closed.

The Indian Presence
1 Emily Carr, *Klee Wyck,* 4.
2 Ibid., 11.
3 See Douglas Cole, *Captured Heritage,* 271.
4 Carr, *Growing Pains,* 211.
5 Totem pole is the term loosely used to refer to a variety of monumental outdoor carvings the natives made: frontal, mortuary, or memorial poles, and sometimes to individual figures like the "welcome man," the D'Sonoqua of the Kwakiutl people, or the mandas—horizontal "catafalque" carvings on which the bodies of chieftains were laid prior to burial. Carr simply spoke of "totem poles" or "poles."
6 Cole, 270.
7 Carr, *Growing Pains,* 211.
8 The material was by Charles Hill-Tout, a Vancouver Salish scholar, and Stephen Denison Peet, who wrote about American Indian religion and mythology. She also had Dr. Newcombe close by for counsel and information.
9 Carr's lecture on Totem Poles is in two notebooks, BCARS.
10 See Arthur Lismer's Article "Art Appreciation" in Brooker, Bertram, ed, *Yearbook of the Arts in Canada 1928–29,* 69.
11 Carr, *Klee Wyck,* 33.
12 *Supplement to the McGill News* (1929), 18, 19.
13 "The Something Plus in a Work of Art," a speech given by Carr 22 October 1935 to the Victoria Normal School students and staff; published in Emily Carr, *Fresh Seeing.*
14 Pearson, 115.
15 Carr, *Hundreds and Thousands,* 28.

16 Carr, *Klee Wyck*, 21.

17 Ibid., 79.

18 Harris to Carr, undated (probably late fall 1929), BCARS.

19 *Supplement, McGill News*, 21.

20 Carr, "The Something Plus in a Work of Art," 37.

21 Carr, *Hundreds and Thousands*, 288.

22 Carr to Nan Cheney, May 1941, Cheney Papers, Special Collections, UBC Library.

23 Carr, *Klee Wyck*, 53.

From Landscape to Nature's Transcendence

1 Carr, *Growing Pains*, 207–08.

2 Carr, Unpublished Journal (1930), BCARS.

3 Carr, *Hundreds and Thousands*. 56.

4 Ibid., 66.

5 Ibid., 106–07.

6 Ibid., 185.

7 Carr to Dilworth, undated (1942 or 1943), BCARS.

8 For an account of this practice see Edythe Hembroff-Schleicher, *m.e. A Portrayal of Emily Carr*, 41–42.

9 Carr to Eric Brown, 4 March 1937, National Gallery.

10 Carr, *Hundreds and Thousands*, 126.

11 See Edythe Hembroff-Schleicher, *The Untold Story*, 126.

12 Carr to Eric Brown, 2 March 1937, National Gallery.

13 See Blanchard, *The Life of Emily Carr*, 198: Edythe Hembroff accompanied her on three occasions.

14 Carr, *Hundreds and Thousands*, 136.

15 Ibid., 134.

16 Ibid., 204.

17 Ibid., 107.

18 Ibid., 132.

19 See particularly Hembroff-Schleicher, *The Untold Story*, 124–43.

20 Ibid., 61.

21 Carr, *Hundreds and Thousands*, 32.

22 Ibid., 61.

23 Ibid., 48.

Afterword

1 Margaret Atwood, *Survival: A Thematic Guide to Canadian Literature* (Toronto: House of Anansi, 1972).

2 Carr, *Hundreds and Thousands*, 101.

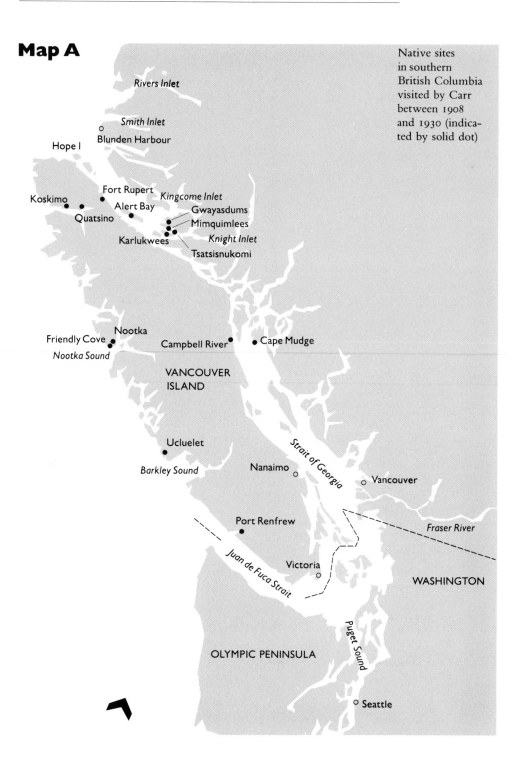

Map A

Native sites
in southern
British Columbia
visited by Carr
between 1908
and 1930 (indica-
ted by solid dot)

Rivers Inlet

Smith Inlet

Blunden Harbour

Hope I

Fort Rupert

Koskimo

Quatsino

Alert Bay

Kingcome Inlet

Gwayasdums

Mimquimlees

Karlukwees

Knight Inlet

Tsatsisnukomi

Nootka

Friendly Cove

Nootka Sound

Campbell River

Cape Mudge

VANCOUVER
ISLAND

Ucluelet

Barkley Sound

Nanaimo

Strait of Georgia

Vancouver

Port Renfrew

Fraser River

Juan de Fuca Strait

Victoria

WASHINGTON

OLYMPIC PENINSULA

Puget Sound

Seattle

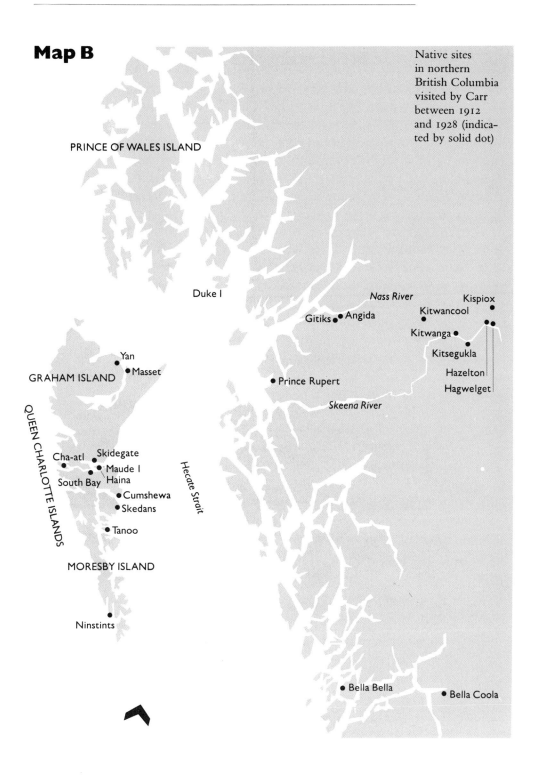

Map B

Native sites in northern British Columbia visited by Carr between 1912 and 1928 (indicated by solid dot)

PRINCE OF WALES ISLAND

Duke I

Nass River

Kispiox

Kitwancool

Gitiks • Angida

Kitwanga

Kitsegukla

Hazelton

Hagwelget

Yan

Masset

GRAHAM ISLAND

QUEEN CHARLOTTE ISLANDS

Prince Rupert

Skeena River

Cha-atl   Skidegate

Maude I

South Bay   Haina

Cumshewa

Skedans

Hecate Strait

Tanoo

MORESBY ISLAND

Ninstints

Bella Bella

Bella Coola

List of Reproductions

Note: Spelling of Indian names has been regularized except where variants have become established through prolonged usage, as in the case of certain titles.

After 1928 Carr dated few works, and locations became less specific. From 1930 the dating of her work is increasingly imprecise.

1899   CEDAR CANIM'S HOUSE, UCLUELET, watercolour, 88

1907   TOTEM WALK AT SITKA, watercolour, 88

1908–09   COMMUNAL HOUSE (Mimquimlees), watercolour, 132

d.1909   GIANT TREES, STANLEY PARK (Vancouver), watercolour, 148

d.1909   Untitled (forest pool with cattle), watercolour, 148

1909 or 1912   ALERT BAY (incorrectly dated 1910), watercolour, 93

d.1909   THE LONE WATCHER (Campbell River), watercolour, 92

1911   AUTUMN IN FRANCE, oil on cardboard, 150

1911   BRITTANY, FRANCE, oil on canvas, 151

1911   BRITTANY LANDSCAPE, oil on cardboard, 150

1911   MENDING THE SAIL, watercolour, 34

1912   ALERT BAY, oil on canvas, 103

1912   ALERT BAY (with Welcome Figure), oil on canvas, 106

1912   CEDAR HOUSE STAIRCASE AND SUNBURST (Mimquimlees), watercolour, 96

1912   POTLATCH FIGURE (Mimquimlees), oil on canvas, 101

c.1912   Untitled (Welcome Figure, Mimquimlees), watercolour, 133

1912   HOUSE POST, TSATSISNUKOMI, watercolour, 93

d.1912   OLD VILLAGE OF GWAYASDUMS, oil on cardboard, 101

d.1912   SKIDEGATE (shark pole), oil on cardboard, 100

d.1912   MAUDE ISLAND TOTEM, oil on cardboard, 100

1912   SKEDANS IN THE RAIN, watercolour, 96

1912   CUMSHEWA, watercolour, 98

1912   CUMSHEWA (with Raven), watercolour, 129

1912   HAIDA TOTEMS, Q.C.I. (Tanoo), watercolour, 99

1912   TANOO, watercolour, 124

d. 1912   VILLAGE OF YAN, Q.C.I., oil on canvas, 103

1912 or
early 1913   VANCOUVER STREET, oil on cardboard, 36

d. 1913   THE WELCOME MAN (Karlukwees), oil on card, 102

1913–15   UNTITLED (trees against whirling sky), oil on canvas, 154

d. 1919   ALONG THE CLIFF, BEACON HILL (Victoria), oil on cardboard, 152

d. 1922   ARBUTUS TREE, oil on canvas, 156

1922–27   Untitled (tree on rocky profile), oil on canvas, 157

1928   KITWANCOOL, graphite drawing, 112

1928   KISPIOX, watercolour, 121

1928   Untitled (Angida), watercolour, 120

1928   NASS RIVER POLE (Gitiks), watercolour, 108

1928   SKEDANS, graphite drawing, 132

1928   SOUTH BAY (Queen Charlotte Islands), watercolour, 108

d. 1928   QUEEN CHARLOTTE ISLANDS TOTEM (Haina), watercolour, 120

1928   SKIDEGATE, oil on canvas, 48

1928   THE CRYING TOTEM (Tanoo), oil on canvas, 121

d. 1928   KITWANCOOL TOTEMS, oil on canvas, 52

1928   Untitled (drawing copied from a Pearson illustration), graphite, 56

1928   KITWANCOOL, watercolour, 119

1928   KITWANCOOL, oil on canvas, 53

1928   Untitled (forest interior), oil on canvas, 54

1929   PORT RENFREW (charcoal drawing), 165

1929   NOOTKA (charcoal drawing), 164

c. 1929   Untitled (stylized island in cartouche), graphite drawing, 160

c. 1929   Untitled (tree rhythms), graphite drawing, 162

c. 1929   Untitled (structured tree forms), graphite drawing, 160

1929   Untitled (tree, drooping branches), graphite drawing, 160

1929   Untitled (formalized trees and foreshore), charcoal drawing, 54

c. 1929   Untitled (South Bay, Q.C.I.), oil on canvas, 158

1929   THE INDIAN CHURCH, FRIENDLY COVE, watercolour, 118

1929   INDIAN CHURCH (Friendly Cove), oil on canvas, 75

1929–30   Untitled (formalized tree forms with totemic details), charcoal drawing,
141

1929–30   Untitled (totemic faces in stylized forest), charcoal drawing, 140

1929–30   WOOD INTERIOR, oil on canvas, 166

1929–30   GREY, oil on canvas, 142

1929–30   NIRVANA (Tanoo), oil on canvas, 124

1929–30   OLD TIME COAST VILLAGE (South Bay), oil on canvas, 136

1929–30   INSIDE A FOREST II, oil on canvas, 54

1929–30   WESTERN FOREST, oil on canvas, 53

c.1930   Untitled ("rhythm, weight, space, force"), graphite drawing, 162

c.1930   Untitled (beach, sea), graphite drawing, 162

1930   Untitled (landscape with "eye" in sky), charcoal drawing, 165

1930   VANQUISHED (Skedans), oil on canvas, 130

1930   POTLATCH WELCOME (Mimquimlees), oil on canvas, 128

1930   INDIAN HUT, QUEEN CHARLOTTE ISLANDS (Cumshewa), oil on canvas, 131

1930   BRITISH COLUMBIA INDIAN VILLAGE (Fort Rupert), oil on canvas, 122

1928–30   THE CROOKED STAIRCASE (Mimquimlees), oil on canvas, 134

c.1930   GUYASDOMS' D'SONOQUA, oil on canvas, 114

1930   AN INDIAN HOUSE, KOSKIMO VILLAGE, watercolour, 110

1930   TERRIBLE TOTEM, KOSKIMO, watercolour, 86

c.1930   Untitled (forest interior, black, grey and white), oil on paper, 177

1930–31   Untitled (trees), oil and charcoal drawing, 177

1929–30   Untitled (cedar tree), charcoal drawing, 168

1931   TREE TRUNK, oil on canvas, 60

1931   CORDOVA DRIFT, oil on canvas, 169

c.1931   SEA DRIFT AT THE EDGE OF THE FOREST, oil on canvas, 158

1931   BIG RAVEN (Cumshewa), oil on canvas, 126

1931   TOTEM AND FOREST (Tow Hill pole, Q.C.I.), oil on canvas, 138

1931   STRANGLED BY GROWTH (Koskimo), oil on canvas, 138

c.1931   DEEP FOREST, oil on canvas, 174

c.1931   A YOUNG TREE, oil on canvas, 172

1931–32   BLUNDEN HARBOUR, oil on canvas, 82

1931–32   OLD AND NEW FOREST, oil on canvas, 74

1931–32   FOREST, BRITISH COLUMBIA, oil on canvas, 76

1931–33   THE RED CEDAR, oil on canvas, 172

1932–33   TREE (spiralling upward), oil on paper, 188

c.1934   STUMPS AND SKY, oil on paper, 189

1932–35   WOOD INTERIOR, oil on canvas, 206

1935   SCORNED AS TIMBER, BELOVED OF THE SKY, oil on canvas, 208

1934–35   METCHOSIN, oil on paper, 200

c.1935–36   Untitled (Clover Point from Dallas Road Beach), oil on paper, 192

1935–36   SKY, oil on paper, 186

1935–36   STUDY IN MOVEMENT, oil on canvas, 184

1935–36   FIR TREE AND SKY, oil on canvas, 199

d.1936   REFORESTATION, oil on canvas, 197

d.1936   SHORELINE, oil on canvas, 169

c.1936   SEASCAPE, oil on paper, 210

1936   YOUNG AND OLD FOREST, oil on paper, 194

1937   ABOVE THE GRAVEL PIT, oil on canvas, 186

1937   SOMETHING UNNAMED, oil on canvas, 194

1937   SWIRL, oil on canvas, 192

1938   YOUNG PINES AND OLD MAPLE, oil on paper, 179

1937–39   ROOTS, oil on canvas, 207

1938–39   CHILL DAY IN JUNE, oil on paper, 209

1938–39   FOREST (tree trunks), oil on paper, 187

1938–39   SELF PORTRAIT, oil on paper, 8

1938–39   SUNSHINE AND TUMULT, oil on paper, 204

1938–40   SOMBRENESS SUNLIT, oil on canvas, 196

c.1939   ROCKS BY THE SEA, oil on paper, 176

c.1939   ABOVE THE TREES, oil on paper, 178

1939   FOREST LANDSCAPE I, oil on paper, 189

1939   HAPPINESS, oil on paper, 190

c.1939   TREES IN THE SKY, oil on canvas, 146

1939–40   DANCING SUNLIGHT, oil on canvas, 198

1941   LAUGHING BEAR (Angida), oil on paper, 144

1941–42   A SKIDEGATE POLE, oil on canvas, 213

c.1942   CEDAR SANCTUARY, oil on paper, 173

d.1942   CEDAR, oil on canvas, 212

d.1942   QUIET, oil on canvas, 212

Selected Bibliography

Appelhof, Ruth S. *The Expressionist Landscape: North American Modernist Painting, 1920–1947*. Birmingham, Ala.: Birmingham Museum of Art, 1988.

Blanchard, Paula. *The Life of Emily Carr*. Vancouver: Douglas & McIntyre, 1987.

Brooker, Bertram, ed. *Yearbook of the Arts in Canada: 1928–1929*. Toronto: Macmillan, 1929.

Carr, Emily. *The Book of Small*. 2nd ed. Toronto: Clarke, Irwin, 1972.

———— *Fresh Seeing: Two Addresses by Emily Carr*. Toronto: Clarke, Irwin, 1972.

———— *Growing Pains*. 1st paperback ed. Toronto: Clarke, Irwin, 1966.

———— *The House of All Sorts*. Centennial ed. Toronto: Clarke, Irwin, 1971.

———— *Hundreds and Thousands: The Journals of Emily Carr*. Toronto: Clarke, Irwin, 1966.

———— *Klee Wyck*. Centennial ed. Toronto, Clarke, Irwin, 1966.

———— "Modern and Indian Art of the West Coast," *Supplement to the McGill News* (June 1929): 18–22.

Cole, Douglas. *Captured Heritage: The Scramble for Northwest Coast Artifacts*. Seattle: University of Washington Press, 1985.

Hembroff-Schleicher, Edythe. *Emily Carr: The Untold Story*. Saanichton, B.C.: Hancock House, 1978.

———— *m.e.: A Portrayal of Emily Carr*. Toronto: Clarke, Irwin, 1969.

Housser, F. B. *A Canadian Art Movement: The Story of the Group of Seven*. Toronto: Macmillan, 1926.

Nasgaard, Roald. *The Mystic North: Symbolist Landscape Painting in Northern Europe and North America 1890–1940*. Toronto: Art Gallery of Ontario, 1984.

Pearson, R. M. *How to See Modern Pictures*. New York: Dial Press, 1928.

Reid, Dennis. *A Concise History of Canadian Painting*. 2nd ed. Toronto: Oxford University Press, 1988.

Seitz, William C. *Mark Tobey*. New York: The Museum of Modern Art, 1962.

Shadbolt, Doris. *The Art of Emily Carr*. Vancouver: Douglas & McIntyre, 1979.

Tippett, Maria. *Emily Carr: A Biography*. Toronto: Oxford University Press, 1979.

Tuchman, Maurice, et al. *The Spiritual in Art: Abstract Painting 1890–1950*. Los Angeles County Museum of Art. New York: Abbeville Press, 1986.

Acknowledgements

The ten years which have passed since *The Art of Emily Carr,* my first book about this extraordinary woman, was published have only added to my estimation of her accomplishment as artist. Inevitably, however, I have come to see various aspects of her evolution in different focus and balance as my perspective has lengthened. Additional original Carr material has become accessible in the interval, and other writers have contributed to the subject. In 1979 when my book came out there existed a substantial list of articles on various aspects of her life and art as well as exhibition reviews and catalogues, but the only substantial work was Edythe Hembroff-Schleicher's *The Untold Story* of 1978, indispensable to Carr students for its chronicling of her exhibiting history and sketching trips. Maria Tippett's biography of Carr was published in 1979 simultaneously with my own book, and a second admirable biography by the American writer Paula Blanchard appeared in 1987. Roald Nasgaard's book on symbolist landscape painting in northern Europe and in North America, which accompanied his 1984 exhibition devoted to the same topic, gave fresh and clear delineation to Carr's place in a broader context of painting. The prominence given to Carr in 1987 by Ruth Appelhof in her exhibition and publication dealing with this continent's modernist landscape painting between 1920 and 1947 similarly permitted the viewing of this artist against a larger background. The fact that two of these authors are American—Blanchard and Appelhof—acknowledges the international appeal and stature of their Canadian subject as person and as artist. Together these four publications have enlarged and refined the field for anyone interested in Carr, as they have for me in undertaking this re-viewing of her work.

I have benefited from the wisdom and perceptive eye of Charles Hill, Curator of Canadian Art at the National Gallery, with whom I have been working on the exhibition of Carr's work that will coincide with the publication of this book. I would also like to acknowledge Glenn Allison's assistance in preparing the chronology. Jerry Mossop, supervisor of the Visual Records Unit of the British Columbia Archives and Records Service and his staff have been infinitely patient with my requests as have been various staff members of the Vancouver Art Gallery. Happily for me Marilyn Sacks was able to undertake the editing of this book as she did of my two previous works. And I am especially grateful to Stoddart Publishing for permission to quote from the published works of Emily Carr, which have been reissued by them.

Index

Italic page numbers indicate reproductions.

ABOVE LAKE SUPERIOR (Harris), 46
ABOVE THE GRAVEL PIT, 185, 186
ABOVE THE TREES, 175, 178
Académie Colarossi, 32
Académie Julian, 26
Alert Bay, 94, 109
ALERT BAY (oil), 97, 103, 105
ALERT BAY (watercolour), 93
ALERT BAY (with Welcome Figure), 106
ALONG THE CLIFF, BEACON HILL, 152, 155
ARBUTUS TREE, 155, 156
ARBUTUS TREE, ESQUIMALT, 38
Armory Exhibition (New York), 49
Art (Clive Bell), 109
art societies, in Canada, 17, 18, 19, 20
art, Canadian, 16
Atkinson, Lawrence, 61
Atwood, Margaret, 215
AUTUMN IN FRANCE, 150, 153
AUTUMN WOODS, 38

Barbeau, Dr. C. Marius, 39, 40, 107
Beacon Hill Park (Victoria), 14, 155, 181
Bell-Smith, F. M., 17
Bella Bella. See northern Kwakiutl
Berkshire (England), 28
BIG PINE, THE, 38
BIG RAVEN, 123, 126, 127, 135, 167
Blake, William, 80, 218
Blavatsky, Helena P., 69, 70, 72–73
BLUNDEN HARBOUR, 82, 113
Book of Small, The, 14, 21, 23
British Columbia (province), 11–12
BRITISH COLUMBIA INDIAN
    VILLAGE, 122, 123
British Columbia Society of Fine
    Arts, 18
Brittany (France), 33, 35
BRITTANY, FRANCE, 33, 151
BRITTANY LANDSCAPE, 37, 150, 153

Brooker, Bertram, 61–62, 66
Brown, Eric, 39, 40, 107
Burchfield, Charles, 62, 63

California School of Design (San
    Francisco), 26
Campbell River, 94
Canadian Art Movement, A (F.
    Housser), 66, 67
Canadian Group of Painters, 19. See
    also, Group of Seven
Canadian Theosophist, 69
"Canadian West Coast Art, Native
    and Modern" (exhibit), 40
Carmichael, Franklin, 41
Carr, Alice, 89
Carr, Emily:
    affinity with other artists, 9, 30,
        63, 97, 155, 205, 217
    art education of (Victoria) 17;
        (San Francisco) 26–27;
        (England) 28–29; (France)
        30–37, 155
    artistic isolation of, 10, 16, 18,
        20, 24, 216
    artistic regeneration of, 39, 42,
        45, 155–59, 216
    awards and exhibitions, 17, 18–
        20, 35–37, 38, 41, 78, 97, 107
    birth and death dates, 10
    collected art. See Emily Carr
        Trust Collection; Newcombe
        Collection
    Canadian outlook of, 10, 14, 216,
        217
    childhood and youth of, 12, 13,
        14, 15, 17
    craftwork of, 105
    cubist idiom, 55, 57, 59, 61, 217
    cultural background of, 10,
        12–13
    empathy with native Indians,
        15–16, 87–89, 104
    fallow period of, 38–39, 105
    fondness for animals, 14–15, 182
    illnesses of, 29–30, 32, 143
    lectures by, 78, 104, 116
    letter writing habits of, 22–23
    major influences on, 23, 41–42,
        45–63
    nature themes of, 26, 28, 29, 33,
        38, 143, 147–214

oil-on-paper technique of, 175, 180–83, 185, 191–195
and photography, 113
Post-Impressionist approach, 28, 33–35, 47, 51, 97, 105, 125, 135, 155, 216, 217
puritanical attitudes of, 14
role of light in paintings, 191, 203
role of movement in paintings, 167–75, 185, 191, 193, 195, 202, 203, 216, 217
sketching trips of, in B.C., 87, 89, 90, 91–95, 109, 111–113, 115, 127, 161, 167, 180–82, 195, 201
spiritual leanings of, 64–66, 67, 68, 69, 70–71, 72–73, 77–81, 125
teaching activities of, 18, 28
travels of, 10, 32, 41, 62, 63, 80
West Coast Indian themes, 15, 30, 39, 40, 41, 83–116, 117–45, 159, 161, 163–67, 211–12, 217
writings of, 21–23. See also *Book of Small; Growing Pains; House of All Sorts; Hundreds and Thousands; Klee Wyck*
Carr, Lizzie, 87
Casson, A. J., 41
CEDAR, 211, *212*
CEDAR CANIM'S HOUSE, UCLUELET, B.C., 87, *88*
CEDAR HOUSE STAIRCASE AND SUNBURST, 95, *96*
CEDAR SANCTUARY, 171, *173*
Cézanne, Paul, 28, 31, 47, 57, 58, 117
CHILL DAY IN JUNE, 205, *209*
COMMUNAL HOUSE (Mimquimlees), *132*
Concarneau (France). See Brittany
CORDOVA DRIFT, *169*, 171
Cornish School of the Arts (Seattle), 49
Crécy-en-Brie (France), 32, 33
CROOKED STAIRCASE, THE, *134*, 135
CRYING TOTEM, THE, (Tanoo), 47, *121*, 123
Cumshewa, 127, 216
CUMSHEWA, *98*
CUMSHEWA (with Raven), *129*

"D'Sonoqua" (story), 111
DANCING SUNLIGHT, *198*
DAWN (Brooker), 62

DAWN OF MAN, THE (Brooker), 62
DEEP FOREST, 171, *174*, 185
Dilworth, Ira, 23
Dove, Arthur, 62, 63, 80
Dreier, Kathleen, 62–63, 78, 79, 218
Drummond Hall (Vancouver), 97
Duchamp, Marcel, 31, 62

Emerson, Ralph Waldo, 66, 79
Emily Carr Trust Collection, 18. *See also* Vancouver Art Gallery
ENDLESS DAWN (Brooker), 62
"Exhibition of Canadian West Coast Art, Native and Modern," 107
"Exhibition of Contemporary Scandinavian Art," 43

Fauvism, 28, 31, 32, 37, 105
Feininger, Arnold, 59
Fergusson, John Duncan, 32
FIR TREE AND SKY, 195, *199*
FOREST, (tree trunks) *187*
FOREST, BRITISH COLUMBIA, 73, *76*, 159, 171
FOREST LANDSCAPE I, *189*
FORSAKEN, 143
Frank, Sophie, 15, 87
Fraser, J. A., 17
"Fresh Seeing" (lecture), 78
Friendly Cove, 161
Fry, Roger, 28

GIANT TREES, STANLEY PARK, *148*, 149
Gibb, Henry Phelan, 31, 32–33, 37
Gitksan people, 94
Goldstream Park and Flats, 167, 181, 201
Graham, Colin, 51
GREY, *142*, 143
Group of Seven 19, 40, 41–44, 45, 63, 66, 67, 68, 72, 77, 78, 80, 135, 155, 159, 217,
Growing Pains: The Autobiography of Emily Carr, 14, 21, 23, 62, 153
Gunther, Dr. Erna, 49
GUYASDOMS' D'SONOQUA, *114*, 125, 127, 135

Haida people, 90, 95
HAIDA TOTEMS, Q.C.I. 95, *99*

Hambidge, Jay, 59
HAPPINESS, *190*
Harris, Lawren, 23, 41, 45, 46, 49, 50, 51, 59, 62, 66, 67–68, 69–70, 71, 72, 73, 77, 80, 116, 135, 161, 163, 193, 218
HAINA, 95, 113
Hill House, 38
Hodgkins, Frances, 35
Hodler, Ferdinand, 10
Holgate, Edwin, 107, 109
HOUSE FRONT, GOLD HARBOUR, 113
House of All Sorts, The, 21, 23, 38
HOUSE POST, TSATSISNUKOMI, *93*
Housser, Bess, 66–67, 70
Housser, Frederick, 66, 68, 70, 79
How To See Modern Pictures (R. Pearson), 57–59, 78, 116–17
Hundreds and Thousands: The Journals of Emily Carr, 22, 40, 65, 72. See also Journals (of Emily Carr)

IN THE PARK, 38
INDIAN CHURCH, 55, 73, 75, 125, 135, 137
INDIAN CHURCH, FRIENDLY COVE, 117, *118*
INDIAN HOUSE INTERIOR, (Tsatsisnukomi) 97
INDIAN HOUSE, KOSKIMO VILLAGE, AN, *110*
INDIAN HUT, QUEEN CHARLOTTE ISLANDS, *131*
INSIDE A FOREST II, *54, 57*
International Exhibition of Modern Art, 62
Island Arts and Crafts Society, 17, 18, 38
Island Art Club. *See* Island Arts and Crafts Society

Jackson, A. Y., 41, 46, 107
Jouillin, Amédée, 26
Journals (of Emily Carr), 77, 79, 125, 201, 202

Kane, Paul, 89, 107
Key to Theosophy, A (H. Blavatsky), 70, 71
Kihn, Langdon, 107
KISPIOX, 117, *121*

KITWANCOOL (drawing), *112*
KITWANCOOL (oil), *53, 55*
KIWANCOOL (watercolour), 117, *119*
KITWANCOOL TOTEMS, *52, 55*
Klee Wyck, 22, 95, 111, 127, 143
Kwakiutl people: southern, 89; northern (Bella Bella), 90

Lamb, Harold Mortimer, 40
LAUGHING BEAR, 143, *144*
Leaves of Grass (Walt Whitman), 79
Léger, Fernand, 30, 57
Lismer, Arthur, 46, 62
LONE WATCHER, THE, *92, 94*

MacDonald, J. E. H., 41
Macdonald, J. W. G., 18
Malevich, Kasimir, 57
Marc, Franz, 63
Martin, T. Mower, 17
Mathews, A. F., 26
MAUDE ISLAND TOTEM, 97, *100*
McCord Museum (Montreal), 94
McGill News, Supplement to the, 107, 115–16
McInnes, G. Campbell, 19
Meadows Studios, Hertfordshire (England), 29
MENDING THE SAIL, *34*
Metchosin, 181, 195
METCHOSIN, *200*
"Modern and Indian Art of the West Coast" (E. Carr), 107
MOVING FORMS (Tobey), *53, 55*
Munch, Edvard, 10, 217

NASS RIVER POLE, *108*
National Gallery Annual Canadian Exhibition (1928), 41
New Art, The (Horace Shipp), 61
Newcombe Collection, 40, 111, 113, 159–61
Newcombe, Dr. C. F., 39–40
Newcombe, William Arnold ("Willie"), 40
Newton, Eric, 19
Nicol, Pegi, 41
NIRVANA, *124,* 125
NOOTKA, *164*
Nootka, 161
Nootka (West Coast people), 89
Northwest Coast Indian culture, 84–85

NUDE DESCENDING THE STAIR
(Duchamp), 62

O'Brien, Lucius, 17
O'Keeffe, Georgia, 62, 80, 217
OLD AND NEW FOREST, 73, *74*
OLD TIME COAST VILLAGE (South
Bay),*136*, 137
OLD VILLAGE OF GWAYASDUMS, 97, *101*
Olsson, Julius, 29
On the Spiritual in Art (Kandinsky), 79

Painters of the Modern Mind (Mary
Cecil Allen), 78
Palmer, Samuel, 218
Patterson, Ambrose, 49
Patterson, Viola, 49
Pearson, Ralph, 163, 167. See also
How to See Modern Pictures
Pemberton, Sophie, 18, 40
Phillips, Walter J., 41
POINT, THE, 38
Port Renfrew, 161
PORT RENFREW, *165*, 167
Post-Impressionism, 31, 33. *See also*
Carr, Post-Impressionist approach
POTLATCH FIGURE (Mimquimlees), *101*
POTLATCH WELCOME
(Mimquimlees), 127, *128*

QUEEN CHARLOTTE ISLANDS
TOTEM, 117, *120*
QUIET, 211, *212*

RED CEDAR, THE, 171, *172*
REFORESTATION, 195, *197*
Reid, Dennis, 38
Richardson, T. J., 89
ROCKS BY THE SEA, *176*
ROOTS, *207*
Royal Academy, 28

St. Efflam (France). *See* Brittany
St. Ives, Cornwall (England), 29
Salish people, 90
Salon d'Automne, 30, 35, 41
Salon des Indépendents, 30
San Francisco Art Association, 27
Savage, Anne, 107
SCHOOLHOUSE, LYTTON, 94
SCORNED AS TIMBER, BELOVED OF
THE SKY, 195, 205, *208*

SEA DRIFT AT THE EDGE OF THE
FOREST, *158*, 159
SEASCAPE, *210*
Seattle Fine Arts Society, 38
SELF PORTRAIT, *8*
Sheeler, Charles, 61
SHORELINE, *169*, 171, 195
Singh, Raja, 71
Skedans, 135
SKEDANS, *132*
SKEDANS IN THE RAIN, 95, *96*
SKIDEGATE, 47, *48*, 97, 123
SKIDEGATE POLE, A, 211, *213*
SKIDEGATE (Shark Pole), *100*
SKY, 185, *186*
Société Anonyme, 62
SOMBRENESS SUNLIT, 195, *196*
"Something Plus in a Work of Art"
(lecture), 78
SOMETHING UNNAMED, *194*, 195
Songhees, 15
SOUTH BAY, *108*, 159
Stieglitz, Alfred, 40, 62
STRANGLED BY GROWTH, *138*, 139
Studio Club (Vancouver), 18
STUDY IN MOVEMENT, *184*, 185
STUMPS AND SKY, *189*
SUNSHINE AND TUMULT, *204*
Survival. See Atwood, Margaret
SWIRL, *192*

Talmage, Algernon, 29
TANOO, *124*, 125
TERRIBLE TOTEM, KOSKIMO, *86*
Tertium Organum (Peter
Ouspensky), 70
Theosophy, 68, 69, 70, 71–73, 77,
80, 85
Thoreau, Henry David, 66
Tlingit people, 90
Tobey, Mark, 45, 47, 49–55, 57, 59,
116, 117, 123, 159, 161, 163, 218
TOTEM AND FOREST, 137, *138*, 139
TOTEM VILLAGE, 113
TOTEM WALK AT SITKA, *88*
Transcendentalism, 80
TREE, *188*
TREES IN THE SKY, *146*
TREE TRUNK, *60*, 61
Tregenna Wood (England), 29
Tsimshian people, 90
Tuchman, Maurice, 65

Ucluelet (Vancouver Island), *87*
Untitled, drawings: (trees and
    foreshore) *54;* (copy from
    Pearson) *56;* (totemic faces,
    forest) *140;* (tree forms, totemic
    details), *141;* (island in cartouche)
    160; (tree forms) *160;* (tree,
    drooping branches) *160;* (beach
    and sea) *162;* (rhythm, weight,
    etc.) *162;* (tree rhythms) *162;*
    (landscape with "eye") *165;*
    (cedar tree) *168*
Untitled, oil on cardboard: (trees) *177*
Untitled, oil on canvas: (forest
    interior) *54;* (trees, whirling sky)
    154; (tree, rocky profile) *157;*
    (South Bay) *158*
Untitled, oil on paper: (forest
    interior) *177;* (Clover Point) *192*
Untitled, watercolours: (Angida)
    120; (Welcome Figure) *133;*
    (forest pool with cattle) *148*
UPLANDS, 38

Vancouver Art Gallery (Carr
    collection), 111, 143, 161, 175
Vancouver School of Decorative
    and Applied Arts, 41
VANCOUVER STREET, 36, 37
Van Gogh, Vincent, 28, 31
VANQUISHED, 125, *130*
Varley, Frederick H., 18, 41, 46
Victoria, 12–13, 16, 17
Victorianism, 13
VILLAGE OF YAN, *103*

WELCOME MAN, THE, *102*
Western Art and the New Era (K.
    Dreier), 63, 78
WESTERN FOREST, *53, 55, 159*
Westminster School of Art, 28, 32
Whiteley, John, 29
Whitman, Walt, 66, 79, 80, 217
WOOD INTERIOR (formalized), *166,
    167, 195*
WOOD INTERIOR (painterly), *206*
Wyle, Florence, 41

Yearbook of the Arts in Canada, 62, 66
YOUNG AND OLD FOREST, *194, 195*
YOUNG PINES AND OLD MAPLE, *179*
YOUNG TREE, A, 171, *172, 185*